Australia

Australia

BY ANN HEINRICHS

Enchantment of the World
Second Series

Children's Press®

A Division of Grolier Publishing

NEW YORK   LONDON   HONG KONG   SYDNEY
DANBURY, CONNECTICUT

Consultant: Michael Corbitt, Library Director, Australian Embassy, Washington, D.C.

Please note: All statistics are as up-to-date as possible at the time of publication.

Visit Children's Press on the Internet: http:/publishing.grolier.com

Book production by Editorial Directions, Inc.
Book design by Ox+Company, Inc.

Library of Congress Cataloging-in-Publication Data

Heinrichs, Ann.
     Australia / by Ann Heinrichs.
     p. cm. — (Enchantment of the world. Second series)
     Includes bibliographical references and index.
Summary: Explores the geography, history, arts, religions, and everyday life of the
     Land Down Under, also called the Lucky Country.
     ISBN 0-516-20648-6
     Australia—Juvenile literature. [1. Australia.] I. Title. II. Series.
     DU96.H45 1998
     994—dc21   98-15780
                                             CIP
                                             AC

Acknowledgments

I am grateful to employees of the Australian National Tourism Office and the Australian consulate for their kind assistance in this project; and to the many Australian people who shared their visions and experiences with me.

Contents

Cover photo:
The Sydney Opera
House

Surfboat racers

A swamp wallaby

The Lucky Country

Danny sits down at the kitchen table in the farmhouse of his family's sheep farm. He flips on the two-way radio and tunes in to Channel Two.

"Good morning, class," says the voice over the crackling speaker. "Open your geography books and turn to Chapter Four."

ANNY FOLLOWS MR. BANKS'S instructions. So do seven other children, some of them more than 1,000 miles (1,600 km) apart.

"Where is Afghanistan?" asks Mr. Banks. Danny presses his "Talk" button, and Mr. Banks's console lights up. He presses the button labeled "Danny."

"It's next to Pakistan, sir. Over."

"Right. When did Afghan people first come to Australia?" Susan, from her trailer home in the western mines, buzzes in.

"In the 1840s. Over."

"Good. Now, what were the Afghans doing here?"

Jimmy answers from Rabbit Flat in the Northern Territory. "Driving the camels, sir. Over."

Point by point, Mr. Banks leads his "class" through the day's lessons. After an hour and a half, it's "over and out" for the day.

A boy takes a class via shortwave radio on Australia's Schools of the Air.

Opposite: **Winter sheep pastures near Mansfield**

Danny and his classmates are students in Australia's Schools of the Air. These long-distance classrooms serve children in remote regions of Australia's outback. Once a year, Danny's class gets together in Alice Springs, where Mr. Banks teaches his daily radio classes. He takes them to his house for a barbecue, and they get to chat with one another face-to-face.

If not for Australia's Schools of the Air, children in remote areas would have little access to formal schooling.

Schools of the Air are just one of the ways people solve the problems of life in the outback. Most of Australia's population is clustered around the coastal cities. There, in the bustling centers of business and culture, people have all the advantages of modern city life.

But Australia is huge. A high-speed, coast-to-coast train trip takes sixty-five hours! Between the coasts lies a vast expanse of bush, range, and desert. Farms such as Danny's sheep station cover more than half the country. In mining regions such as Susan's, a day's drive might reach one scraggly town. And, until the 1930s, people really did use camels to cross the great deserts of the interior.

For native Aboriginal people, life in these desolate stretches came naturally. For more than 40,000 years, they

Geopolitical map of Australia

Today's native Aboriginal children have more opportunities for an education than their parents did.

The Bush and the Outback

Australians call any natural place outside the city the "bush." When someone is 'way out—truly far from population centers—they're in the "outback."

worked with a harsh climate and unforgiving land. They knew their way around. They knew every plant, animal, and waterhole and taught their children the Earth's secrets.

Then the white people arrived, and a new era began. Australia would never be the same. Founded as a British prison colony, the island continent grew into a thriving settlement of farms and mines. Its six separate colonies joined under a central government in 1901.

For outsiders, Australia seems to cast an enchanting spell. Some see it as a land of cuddly koalas and leaping kangaroos. Others think it's a land of intrepid bush men such as the knife-toting Crocodile Dundee. But a typical Australian might say it's the land of footie and barbies—football and barbecues!

One of Australia's nicknames is the Lucky Country. On the brink of the twenty-first century, a lot of Australians hope to collect on that luck. Natives are winning back their land rights, and the government is pushing to become a full-fledged republic.

Danny and his classmates are sure to be lucky, too. With the help of Mr. Banks, they won't miss a single detail. Over and out!

The Land Down Under

For ancient Europeans, most of the known world lay in the Northern Hemisphere. Some people, however, believed that the southern half of the Earth must hold vast lands and civilizations, too. Around A.D. 150, the Greek geographer Ptolemy drew a now-famous map of the world. It included a great continent in the south. Ptolemy labeled it *Terra Australis Incognita*— Latin for "Unknown Southern Land." Australia eventually got its name from the Latin word *Australis* meaning "southern."

Opposite: **One of Ptolemy's maps of the world.**

ONE OF AUSTRALIA'S NICKNAMES IS THE LAND DOWN Under—down under the equator, that is. Because it lies in the Southern Hemisphere, its seasons are the opposite of those on the northern half of the globe.

Australia is an island between the South Pacific Ocean and the Indian Ocean. It's two islands, really. Tasmania, off the southeast coast, was once joined to the mainland.

An aerial view of Sydney

Australia is not only a country. It's also a continent—the smallest of Earth's seven great landmasses.

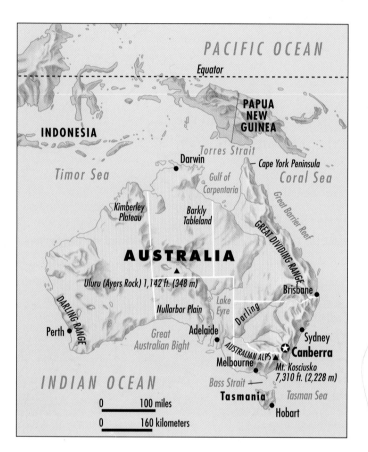

Topographical map of Australia

Several other island nations are very close to Australia. Just to the north are Papua New Guinea, Indonesia, and part of Malaysia. A little farther north are the Philippines and the Asian mainland. Southeast of Australia is New Zealand. Like Australia, it was once a British colony. To the south is the icy continent of Antarctica.

Geological History

Most geologists believe that all the land on Earth was once a single landmass called *Pangaea,* which is Greek for "all the Earth." Around 200 million years ago, Pangaea began to split in two. The southern "chunk" of Pangaea became Gondwanaland. Over time, Gondwanaland broke up, forming the continents of Australia, Africa, South America, and Antarctica and the subcontinent of India. Finally, Australia and Antarctica went their separate ways. Antarctica drifted to the South Pole, while Australia moved closer to the equator.

The Eastern Highlands

The eastern edge of Australia is the Eastern Highlands region, the nation's best farmland. The region runs all the way down the east coast from northern Queensland's Cape York Peninsula to southern Tasmania. Before land was cleared for cities and farms, lush rain forests covered the highlands. Some of these rain forests still stand in unsettled parts of the east coast.

Ellis Beach, on the eastern coast of Queensland

Along the Pacific Ocean is a low plain with beaches and jagged cliffs. Australia's heaviest population centers are on the east and southeast coasts. They include Brisbane, Sydney, and Melbourne. Canberra, the capital, is slightly inland.

The Great Dividing Range runs parallel to the entire east coast. It's not really a mountain range but a stretch of hills and plateaus covered with grasslands and forests. Australia's highest mountains—the Australian Alps—rise at the south end of the Great Dividing Range. Australians and tourists from around the world love to ski in the Snowy Mountains,

Skiing is a favorite sport on the southern slopes of the Australian Alps

the highest range in the Alps. Australia's tallest peak, Mount Kosciusko, rises in the Snowies.

The island of Tasmania is part of the Great Dividing Range, too. A land bridge once connected it to the mainland. Now the Bass Strait flows between the two. Southwestern Tasmania is a wilderness of rugged mountains, river rapids, and thundering waterfalls.

The tiny Torres Strait Islands are scattered in the far northeast of Australia, just off Queensland's Cape York Peninsula. They include Thursday Island, Prince of Wales Island, and Possession Island.

The Central Lowlands

Beyond the Great Dividing Range are the Central Lowlands. They extend from the Gulf of Carpentaria in the north to the southeast coast of South Australia. Rain falls in the far north and the far south, but the lowlands are generally arid. Most crops cannot grow in this dry soil, but cattle ranchers graze their animals on the tough grass and scrubby shrubs of the lowlands.

The low, desolate Simpson Desert covers the western part of the lowlands, toward the center of the country. In northern South Australia, the dry beds of salt lakes stretch to the horizon. Among them is Lake Eyre, Australia's lowest point at 52 feet (16 m) below sea level.

The giant Wave Rock is an amazing structure created by nature.

The Great Western Plateau

The high, flat Great Western Plateau covers the western two-thirds of Australia. Crops grow well in the far north and the southwest because of plentiful rainfall. A low plain lines the seacoast. Herds of cattle and sheep graze farther inland, where the land is hilly and grassy. As on the east coast, the biggest cities are the seaports. Perth is the largest of the coastal cities.

East of Perth is a 200-million-year-old rock formation called Wave Rock. Its arched shape and colorful granite stripes make it look like a giant wave. Deep

Kakadu National Park

Kakadu National Park is in Arnhem Land, at the "Top End" of the Northern Territory. It lies about 150 miles (241 km) east of Darwin. Kakadu is the largest national park in Australia and the third largest in the world. Its name comes from *Gagadju,* a local Aboriginal tribe. Aboriginals have lived in this area for at least 25,000 years. They lease Kakadu to the National Parks and Wildlife Service and take part in managing it.

On the north edge of Kakadu are mangrove swamps and rain forests. Inland, the landscape is natural and wild. Some of the ancient Aboriginal rock paintings that adorn Nourlangie Rock, Ubirr Rock, and other sites are over 20,000 years old. Jabiru storks, crocodiles, and wallabies are among the thousands of species of wildlife. Much of the movie *Crocodile Dundee* was filmed in Kakadu.

gorges in vivid colors run through Hamersley Range National Park in the Pilbara region. In the far northwestern Kimberleys, Bungle Bungle National Park features spectacular rock pillars, beehives, and domes. Vast expanses of desert take up the central part of the plateau—the Great Sandy Desert in the north, the Gibson Desert in the center, and the Great Victoria Desert to the south.

At the Northern Territory's "Top End" are Arnhem Land and the city of Darwin. Farther south is the Tanami Desert. In the "Red Centre" is massive Ayers Rock and the town of Alice Springs. Aboriginal Reserves cover much of central Australia.

Ayers Rock

Ayers Rock—*Uluru* to the Aborigines—is a massive rock formation in the desolate center of Australia. Iron oxide in the sandstone gives Ayers Rock its blazing, red-orange color. The rock rises 1,142 feet (348 m) above the surrounding desert, but scaling it is a 1-mile (1.6-km) climb. A trek around its base is a 6-mile (9.7-km) hike. *Uluru,* meaning "shadowy place," is sacred to the Aboriginals. The area was returned to Mutijulu Aboriginals in 1985, and they manage it jointly with Australia's National Parks and Wildlife Service.

Along the southern coast is the Nullarbor Plain. Nullarbor, meaning "no trees" in Latin, is a good name for this arid plateau. East of the plain, set in a bay, is the city of Adelaide.

States and Territories

Australia is carved into six states and two mainland territories. Almost all their borders are perfectly straight, drawn along lines of latitude and longitude. From largest to smallest,

A small suburban community nestled alongside a harbor in New South Wales

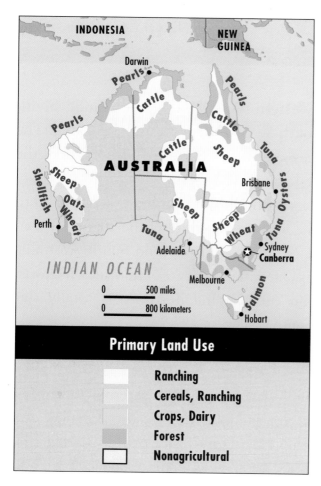

Primary Land Use

- Ranching
- Cereals, Ranching
- Crops, Dairy
- Forest
- Nonagricultural

Geographical Features

Area: 2,978,147 square miles (7,713,364 sq km)

Highest Elevation: Mount Kosciusko, 7,310 feet (2,228 m)

Lowest Elevation: Lake Eyre, 52 feet (16 m) below sea level

Longest River: Darling River, 1,702 miles (2,739 km)

Largest City: Sydney

the states are Western Australia, Queensland, South Australia, New South Wales, Victoria, and Tasmania. The mainland territories are the Northern Territory and the Australian Capital Territory (Canberra).

It's easy to learn the layout of Australia. Western Australia covers the western one-third of the country. Down the center are the Northern Territory and South Australia. The eastern third is Queensland, New South Wales, Victoria, and Tasmania. The tiny Capital Territory is totally surrounded by New South Wales.

The External Territories

Australia also claims several so-called external territories. Four of them have a population of zero: the Ashmore and Cartier Islands, the Heard and McDonald Islands, the Australian Antarctic Territory, and the Coral Sea Islands.

About 800 people live on Christmas Island, and Norfolk Island has more than 2,000 residents. A few hundred people live on the Cocos (Keeling) Islands.

The Great Barrier Reef

Many a ship has been smashed to bits on the Great Barrier Reef. This string of rock-hard islands curves around Queensland's northeast coast for some 1,250 miles (2,012 km). The surrounding waters are called the Coral Sea. Strangely enough, this reef—the scene of so much death and destruction —is made almost entirely of skeletons!

Sailors navigate carefully in the waters near the Great Barrier Reef.

Looking at the State Capitals

Sydney, the capital of New South Wales, is Australia's oldest and largest city. It surrounds Sydney Harbour, with its famous landmarks—the Sydney Opera House and Sydney Harbour Bridge. The bridge leads to the Rocks, where Australia's first settlers landed in 1788. That area is now Sydney's Old Town. The city center, Australia's economic hub, is built around Hyde Park. Looming over it all is Sydney Tower, the tallest building in the Southern Hemisphere.

Melbourne (above), the capital of Victoria, grew up around the Yarra River. Its metropolitan area is enormous, and much of it is devoted to gardens and parks. A multi-cultural city, Melbourne is home to many European and Asian peoples—and their arts and food. Among the modern buildings, many beautiful old structures remain from the mining boom of the 1850s.

Brisbane (opposite, right), the capital of Queensland, straddles the Brisbane River. The city's Queensland Arts Centre, a cluster of ultramodern buildings, stands alongside beautiful structures from earlier times, such as City Hall, the Old Government House, and the Post Office. The international exhibition Expo 88 took place on Brisbane's South Bank Parkland.

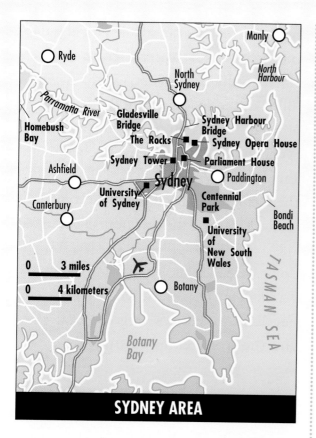

SYDNEY AREA

Perth, the capital of Western Australia, sits at the mouth of the Swan River on the Indian Ocean. Perth is the business and shipping center for the state's mining industries. Gleaming office buildings tower over the city center, while elegant colonial buildings line St. George's Terrace. Perth's attractions include the Tudor-style buildings of London Court, the Cultural Centre, and King's Park.

Adelaide, the capital of South Australia, has been called the "city of churches." Now modern high-rise buildings overshadow the settlers' churches and stone houses. The River Torrens flows through Adelaide, and lush parks and gardens surround the city. Shoppers flock to Rundle Mall, and Festival Centre hosts the biennial Adelaide Arts Festival.

Hobart, the capital of Tasmania, is Australia's southernmost city. It sits at the foot of Mount Wellington, where the Derwent River meets the Tasman Sea. Hobart, Australia's second settlement, was an important whaling port in the early days. Guns at Battery Point once guarded the harbor. Old warehouses are now shops along the cobblestone streets of Salamanca Place. The Tasmanian Museum and Art Gallery and the Maritime Museum cover the area's culture and history.

For millions of years, tiny sea creatures called coral polyps lived off Australia's northeast coast. After a polyp died, its porous skeleton remained on the ocean floor. Gradually, minerals in the seawater filled in the spaces where the polyp's soft tissue had been. Over time, the skeletons became as hard as rock. With each new generation, living polyps attached themselves to the older, bony layers.

Layer after layer, the reef built up until the highest mounds rose above the ocean surface. Spying the reef from afar, a navigator might think it was a patch of sandbars. But even a slight collision could rip a gaping hole in a ship's hull—and the visible part of the reef is only a small fraction of the whole rocky mass.

The Great Barrier Reef is Earth's largest coral reef. Scientists from around the world come to study its exotic

After the tide goes out, the beautiful but treacherous coral of the Great Barrier Reef is exposed.

World Heritage Sites

The United Nations Educational, Scientific, and Cultural Organization (UNESCO) has selected certain places around the globe as World Heritage sites. The sites are chosen for their natural, historic, or archaeological value. Australia has thirteen World Heritage sites: the Great Barrier Reef, Kakadu National Park, the Willandra Lakes Region, the Tasmanian Wilderness, the Lord Howe Island Group, Uluru-Kata Tjuta National Park, the Australian East Coast Temperate and Sub-Tropical Rainforest Parks, the Wet Tropics of Queensland, Shark Bay in Western Australia, Fraser Island, Riversleigh/Naracoorte Mammal Fossil Sites, Heard and McDonald Islands, and Macquarie Island.

animal and plant life. Pollution and tourism, however, have destroyed many other coral reefs, and the Great Barrier Reef is feeling the impact, too. The Australian government and international conservation agencies are working to preserve this natural treasure.

Australia's tropical region
in Queensland

Climate

Almost half of Australia—the northern part of the country—
lies in the Earth's tropical zone. The tropics are a broad band
of land just north and south of the equator—the warmest
regions on Earth. The southern boundary of the tropical zone
is an east–west line called the Tropic of Capricorn. It runs
across Australia, passing just north of Alice Springs.

Australia's tropical region is warm to hot all year. Weather
in the far north is typical of the tropics, with a "wet" season
(November to April) and a "dry" season (May to October). The

southern part of the country has a temperate climate. Like most of the United States, it has four distinct seasons. Summers are warm and winters are cold. Remember, though, that July is midwinter for Australians, and January is midsummer!

The vast desert regions are arid, with only rare rainfall. Their biggest temperature contrasts are the hot days and cool nights. Australia's heaviest rains fall along the north, east, and southeast coasts. Queensland's coast is drenched with about 150 inches (381 cm) of rain every year. Snow is rare. Only the Australian Alps and parts of Tasmania get regular snowfalls.

One of Australia's vast arid regions in the west

The wet season brings violent rainstorms and cyclones on the north coast and floods farther inland. Droughts are common throughout much of Australia and can be devastating to the nation's economy. Crops shrivel and grasses die, leaving sheep and cattle without enough to eat. With the droughts come wildfires. What's to blame for the dry weather? These days, a lot of people are blaming El Niño.

El Niño

El Niño, Spanish for "the child," refers to the baby Jesus. South Americans picked the name because El Niño often strikes their coastal waters around Christmas.

Just what *is* El Niño? It's an unusual shifting of warm Pacific Ocean waters. Normally, those waters stay in the western Pacific, near Asia. But in an "El Niño year," they head east, toward the Americas. This shift occurs once every two to seven years. El Niño makes the land on the western Pacific Rim unusually hot and dry. On the eastern edge of the Pacific, it has the opposite effect—bringing unusually cool weather and torrential rains. On the U.S. Pacific coast, for example, El Niño drenches the state of California with some of the worst of these rainstorms.

El Niño showed up again in 1997–1998. Scientists believe it caused Australia's devastating drought that season. The wildfires that came with it ravaged millions of acres of forest and grassland.

Wild Things

Some of the strangest animals in the world live in Australia. And many of them live nowhere else *but* Australia. For instance, Australia is the only place on Earth where you'd find kangaroos, koalas, and platypuses in the wild. Why is this? Why do so many unique species live down under?

Opposite: **Many creatures resemble the environment in which they live.**

THE ANSWER LIES IN THE CONTINENT'S geological history. When Australia was part of Gondwanaland, its animals were very like others on that great landmass. When Australia broke away, its animals came with it. Separated from their relatives, they evolved in completely different ways.

Marsupials

Kangaroos and koalas are probably the best-known Australian animals. Both are marsupials—a type of mammal. When a marsupial is born, it's only a tiny embryo. A baby kangaroo, or joey, is about 1 inch (2.5 cm) long at birth. The embryo grows inside a pouch on its mother's belly until it's ready to live on its own. Australia is home to about 260 species of marsupials, including wallabies, moles, bandicoots, wombats, and possums. (Possum is the usual Australian word for opossum.) Wallabies are a

The National Animals

Australia's two national animals are the kangaroo and the emu. They appear on either side of the crest on Australia's national coat of arms. Large kangaroos run up to 30 miles (48 km) an hour. In a running leap, they can broad-jump 30 feet (9 m).

The emu is the world's second-largest bird, after the ostrich. It stands 5 to 6 feet (1.5 to 1.8 m) tall and weighs as much as 130 pounds (59 kg). Like kangaroos, emus can run up to 30 miles (48 km) an hour. They can swim, too. After the female lays her eggs, the male sits on them till they hatch.

Funny Noses, Runny Noses

The koala looks like a cuddly teddy bear with a rather large nose. It's sometimes called Australia's native bear. But it's not a bear at all—it's a marsupial. Koalas inhabit the eastern forests and eat the leaves of eucalyptus trees. They sleep in the daytime and eat at night, consuming about 2.5 pounds (1.1 kg) of leaves a day. Koalas are prone to diseases and often get colds and runny noses, just as people do. Once hunted almost to extinction, koalas are now protected by law. Some zoos have koala adoption programs that let people take a koala home and raise it as part of the family.

type of kangaroo. They live on the open grasslands, while marsupial moles burrow into the desert sand. Bandicoots are small, ratlike creatures, and wombats look like little bears.

A common wombat

Kangaroos

About 50 kinds of kangaroo live in Australia. They range from the rabbit-size rat kangaroo to the 5-foot (1.5-m) great red kangaroo of the inland plains. The tree kangaroo of the rain forest has thick claws for climbing trees. The kangaroo seen in most zoos is the great grey kangaroo.

The swamp wallaby, a type of kangaroo

In some areas, kangaroos are so numerous that they're regarded as pests. After they eat up the food supply in the bush, they dine on farmers' crops and even on lawns. Passionate arguments rage on the kangaroo issue. Some people favor controlled hunting of kangaroos. This cuts down the kangaroo population so that the remaining animals get enough to eat.

Some kangaroos species are killed for their hides and meat. In the early 1990s, states began to legalize the selling of kangaroo meat in supermarkets. This outraged the people who feel it is wrong to kill kangaroos for any reason.

The platypus is native to Tasmania and southern and eastern Australia.

Egg-Laying Mammals

A major difference between mammals and other animals is that mammals are born live, rather than hatched from eggs. But two Australian animals break that rule—the duck-billed platypus and the echidna. They are the only egg-laying mammals in the world. Scientists call them monotremes.

Platypuses live in burrows on riverbanks. They eat grub worms and aquatic animals such as shrimp. Their bills help them to catch food as they swim underwater. Echidnas have long claws, long snouts, and quills like a porcupine's. They may live to be fifty years old. The female lays her eggs, then grows a pouch to keep the hatchlings in until they're big enough to make it on their own.

Dangerous Creatures

Some of Australia's most dangerous creatures are reptiles. The crocodile that lives along the northern coast is a fearsome, flesh-eating reptile. It may grow to 15 feet (4.6 m) or longer. Its freshwater relative, however, poses no threat to humans. Measuring only about 8 feet (2.4 m), it feeds on water plants, fish, and other small water animals.

Pythons, Australia's largest snakes, grow as long as 24 feet (7.3 m). They wrap themselves around their prey, squeeze it to death, and then swallow it whole. It may take days or even weeks for a python to digest an animal. Dogs, cattle, and even humans have fallen prey to pythons' deadly attacks. Reports from the bush tell of pythons that have died because a victim was simply too large to get through the snake's digestive system.

An alert green tree python

In all, Australia has about 170 species of snake, and many of them are poisonous. Those with the deadliest venom are the taipan, the tiger snake, and the death adder.

Most of Australia's lizards are harmless, but some can look quite scary. When it's alarmed, the frilled lizard unfurls its big, fanlike collar, stands up on its hind legs, and prances away at high speed. Goannas, which belong to a large lizard family of the Australian bush, may bite if they're annoyed. "Goanna" is a version of the word "iguana," but they are actually monitor lizards that range in length from 12 to 29 inches (30 to 74 cm). Thorny devils and geckos are other common lizards.

Dingoes and Tasmanian Devils

The dingo is Australia's wild dog. Aborigines once tamed dingoes as pets, but today they are serious predators. Dingoes prey on sheep and other livestock, and they are sometimes bold enough to attack huge kangaroos. A dingo-proof barrier called the Wild Dog Fence ranks as the longest fence in the world. It stretches almost 3,300 miles (5,311 km) from southeast Queensland to South Australia's seacoast.

Tasmanian devils look cute on Saturday-morning cartoons, but some say they're Australia's meanest, toughest

Dingoes pose serious problems to livestock owners.

animals. Their powerful bite inflicts an awful wound. They eat every last bit of their prey—bones, hair, and all. Tasmanian devils live only in Tasmania. They're nocturnal marsupials, feeding by night and sleeping by day.

The Camels' Tale

Australia is the only country where camels run wild. (They're also called dromedaries and have one hump; Bactrian camels have two humps.) Australia's camels graze on grass and shrubs and also eat tree leaves and fruit. Adult camels need at least 4.2 ounces (119 g) of salt a day, so camels are often seen around salt lakes. They sometimes crash through farmers' fences to get to the watering troughs.

Some of Australia's wild camels are trained to work in supply caravans.

Termite Castles

The chunky brown towers that rise from the landscape in some desert regions are termite "castles." Some of them are 20 feet (6 m) tall. Termites, called white ants, build these nests by secreting digested plant material. The magnetic termite, a species found near Darwin, knows its directions. It builds its nest with the longest part along a north-south axis.

Camels were introduced to Australia from North Africa and the Middle East to explore and develop the arid desert lands. They led explorers through the desert, pulled plows, and carted supplies for railroad-building crews. One lone camel was shipped to South Australia in 1840, and more than 100 others arrived in 1866. Later, about 4,500 camels were brought in to work in the western goldfields.

Some of these camels escaped into the wild. Exploring expeditions lost camels or left them behind. More and more camels were released in the 1920s and 1930s as motor vehicles took their place. Now thousands of wild camels roam across Australia's deserts. The agriculture department is looking for ways to put them to good use.

Animal Imports

Europeans brought dozens of new animal species to Australia. Some were farm animals, such as sheep, cattle, and goats, but settlers also brought foxes, cats, and rabbits.

Rabbits arrived in Australia in the mid-1800s. They multiplied quickly, overrunning sheep and cattle pastures.

Rabbit-proof fences helped a little, but farmers brought rabbits under control only by spreading a fatal rabbit disease.

Some settlers brought their pet cats to Australia. As litter after litter were born, the cats ran off and became feral (wild). Now Australia's wild cats are serious predators, cutting down the populations of many birds and small mammals. Imported foxes became predators, too.

Cane toads came to Queensland in the 1930s. Farmers brought these "killer" toads from Hawaii to rid the sugarcane plantations of beetles. Moving on from the sugarcane fields, the toads multiplied in the wild. They're big enough to eat small animals, and their bodies contain a deadly poison that discourages predators.

A kookaburra

The crimson rosella, a type of parrot, is commonly found in Queensland, Victoria, and Tasmania.

Birds

Australia is home to about 700 species of birds. Emus and cassowaries are among the largest. Like ostriches, neither of these birds can fly. Australia is the only place in the world where the black swan lives. The kookaburra, a relative of the kingfisher, emits a rasping, raucous cackle that earned it the nickname "laughing jackass."

In the tropical forests, brilliantly colored parrots and cockatoos screech and flit overhead. Parakeets, lorikeets, budgerigars, and zebra finches are other colorful—and noisy—species. They often travel in huge flocks. The lyrebird, named for its long, gracefully curved plumes, was once hunted for its feathers. Today, the lyrebird is a protected species. Occasionally it uses its short wings for normal flight. But most of the time, a lyrebird takes flying jumps from rock to rock and tree to tree.

Along the coast, familiar birds are cranes, ducks, geese, spoonbills, and pelicans. Dwarf penguins are found on the southern coast and in Tasmania.

Life on the Great Barrier Reef

The Great Barrier Reef is alive with dazzling colors and bizarre shapes. More than 1,500 species of fish dart in and out of the coral. They include surgeon fish, butterfly fish, lionfish, angelfish, clownfish, and blue tangs. Groupers and sharks are among the large predators. About 400 species of coral live

Beautiful sea anemones live on the coral reefs.

there, too. Staghorn coral and brain coral look like their names. A brain coral can live for more than 100 years.

Other reef residents are sea anemones, sea urchins, sea snails, lobsters, prawns, jellyfish, manta rays, and giant clams. And there are dugongs, large mammals similar to manatees. Natives of nearby islands visit the reef to collect scallops and other shellfish.

Seabirds swoop over the coral islands and dive for fish while herons and other shorebirds wade on the shallow banks. Sea turtles lay their eggs on some of the islands, too. Once hunted for food, the turtles are now a protected species.

Trees, Shrubs, and Grasses

Towering trees grow in dense rain forests on the east coast and in the far southwest. Farther inland, trees are shorter and farther apart. They stand among low shrubs and grasses that are good for grazing. Over time, farmers have cleared these woodlands to free more pasture for cattle and sheep.

Deeper in the interior there is scrubland, covered with tough-leaved bushes. As the land becomes more arid, grasses take over and the scrub becomes more sparse. A stiff, sharp-leaved grass called spinifex grows in some desert regions. Termites eat spinifex and process it into material for building their castles.

It's easy to tell when you're near a stand of eucalyptus trees—you can smell them. The leaves secrete an oil with a sharp, almost medicinal odor. The eucalyptus is the dominant tree of the continent. Australians call it the gum tree.

The National Floral Emblem

The golden wattle, a type of acacia, is Australia's national floral emblem. It's a golden-blossomed shrub or small tree that grows in the forest underbrush and scrublands of southeastern Australia. Golden wattles appear on Australia's coat of arms. On September 1, National Wattle Day, people are encouraged to plant an acacia.

There are more than 500 species of eucalyptus throughout the country. Some are trees and some are shrubs. In the rain forests, eucalyptus trees grow as high as 200 feet (61 m). Shrub species grow in the drier scrublands. The locals call them mallee. Acacias, known as wattles, are common plants in the interior. They, too, have developed several hundred species.

Human Tracks

Humans first arrived in Australia at least 40,000 years ago. They migrated from Southeast Asia, either by boat or over land bridges. These people were the ancestors of Australia's Aboriginal population. The climate changed drastically over thousands of years, becoming hotter and drier, but the people adapted to changing conditions and survived.

Before Europeans arrived, between 300,000 and 1 million Aboriginals inhabited the continent. They lived in tribal groups scattered throughout Australia. Each tribe was made up of clans of several families. These native people hunted animals and gathered edible plants. They ate roots, tubers, and wild fruits, as well as kangaroos, possums, lizards, fish, and shellfish. When wild game thinned out in one area, the clan moved to another spot.

Spiritual beliefs guided their way of life. The Aboriginals believed that mythical beings created the world and bestowed fertility and power. These beings belonged to a spiritual realm called the Dreaming. Through dances and rituals, the Aboriginals kept in touch with the Dreaming beings and thus gained strength and wisdom.

A painting of Europeans on Van Diemen's Land by Captain George Tobin, 1792

The First Europeans

Willem Jansz, a Dutch navigator, was the first European known to set foot on Australia. In 1606, he landed on what is now Cape York Peninsula in the

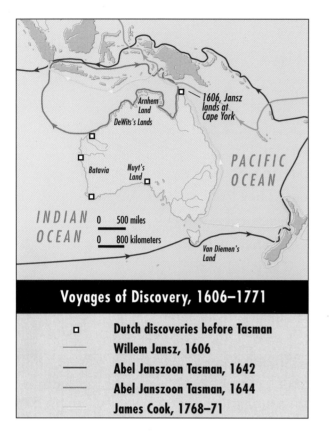

Voyages of Discovery, 1606–1771

☐	**Dutch discoveries before Tasman**
——	**Willem Jansz, 1606**
——	**Abel Janszoon Tasman, 1642**
——	**Abel Janszoon Tasman, 1644**
	James Cook, 1768–71

northeast. But Jansz had no idea he had landed in the mysterious southern continent. At the time, he thought he was in New Guinea.

Dutch seamen on a ship named the *Arnhem* explored Australia's northern coast in 1623 and named the area Arnhem Land—a name that survives today. Another Dutchman, Abel Janszoon Tasman, was sure he had found the Unknown Southern Land. On a voyage in 1642, he sighted land, stepped ashore, and called the place Van Diemen's Land. (Antonij Van Diemen was the Dutch governor of Batavia— now Djakarta, Indonesia. Today, Van Diemen's Land is called Tasmania.)

Captain Cook

Captain James Cook was on a secret mission for Great Britain's Royal Navy. In 1770, he sailed his ship, the *Endeavour*, into a bay on Australia's east coast. With him was the botanist, or plant scientist, Sir Joseph Banks. Banks was so dazzled by the marvelous plant life that he named the area Botany Bay.

Cook continued exploring the coast, naming various land features as he went along. After four months, he fulfilled the goal of his mission: claiming all of eastern

Captain Cook

Captain James Cook (1728–1779) of the British Royal Navy made several voyages of exploration and discovery. He explored North America's St. Lawrence River in 1759 and later mapped the coasts of Newfoundland and Labrador. In 1769, he led an expedition to Tahiti in the *Endeavour,* then mapped the coasts of New Zealand, Australia, and New Guinea. He was shipwrecked on the Great Barrier Reef. After repairs, he landed on what is now Possession Island and, on August 22, 1770, claimed eastern Australia for England. Then he returned, having sailed around the whole globe. On a later voyage, Cook completed another circumnavigation of the Earth. He was killed by Hawaiian natives on a third attempt.

Australia for King George III of England. He named it New South Wales.

In the late eighteenth century, Great Britain's jails were bursting at the seams. One way to relieve this problem was to send shiploads of prisoners out to the British colonies. But the American colonies had fought their way to independence by 1783. That left Great Britain with too many prisoners and nowhere to put them. New South Wales was the perfect solution to the prison problem.

A detail of Australia and Cook's travels, from Daniel F. Sotzmann's drawing of the world, 1792

In 1787, Captain Arthur Phillip set sail from England with a fleet of eleven ships. On board were 730 convicts—570 men and 160 women. They were to form the backbone of the new colony. To keep them in line, there were about 200 British soldiers. Some officers brought their wives and children, too.

Phillip landed at Botany Bay on January 18, 1788. On January 26, a few miles up the coast, he and his passengers disembarked at Sydney Cove and began their new life. Now the city of Sydney, this was the first European settlement in Australia. Australians celebrate January 26 as National Day.

Other penal colonies followed. Convicts cleared and farmed the land and built houses and buildings for the colonial government. When a convict's prison term was up, he or she was set free. Until then, discipline was severe. Naturally, not everyone could stand to wait out the term. Lucky escapees disappeared into the bush and were never found. Some became bushrangers, or bandits.

Freed convicts and military officers were given land to farm. Many of them raised sheep and exported

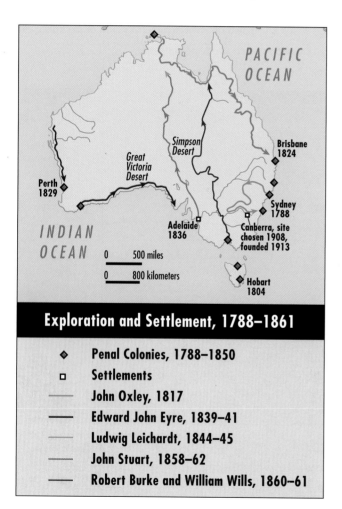

Exploration and Settlement, 1788–1861

◆ **Penal Colonies, 1788–1850**
□ **Settlements**
— **John Oxley, 1817**
— **Edward John Eyre, 1839–41**
— **Ludwig Leichardt, 1844–45**
— **John Stuart, 1858–62**
— **Robert Burke and William Wills, 1860–61**

An engraving of Phillip's fleet entering Botany Bay

the wool to England. By law, the colonial government owned all of Australia's wide-open spaces. But the law couldn't control farmers who were hungry for more land. Some, called squatters, simply moved onto a nice expanse of land and began farming it. In time, they became some of Australia's biggest landowners.

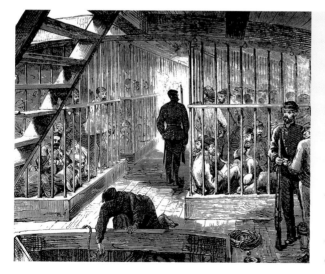

Convicts

On their voyage from England to Australia, convicts were crammed into the ship's lower deck among bugs and rats. Conditions were filthy, disease was rampant, and many prisoners died on the way. Those who survived faced back breaking labor and brutal treatment in the prison colonies. In all, about 160,000 convicts were transported to Australia over a period of eighty years. New South Wales became so glutted with convicts that the governor refused to take any more after 1848. Western Australia continued to accept convicts until 1868, when Britain ended the transportations.

Return of Burke and Wills to Cooper's Creek,
by Nicolas Chevalier, 1868

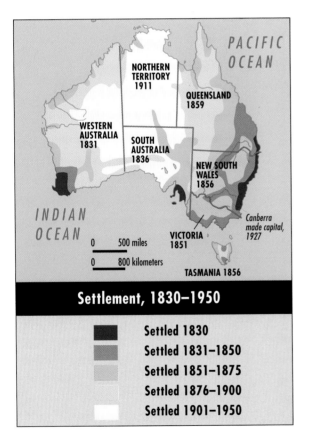

PACIFIC
OCEAN

NORTHERN
TERRITORY
1911

QUEENSLAND
1859

WESTERN
AUSTRALIA
1831

SOUTH
AUSTRALIA
1836

NEW SOUTH
WALES
1856

INDIAN
OCEAN

0   500 miles

0   800 kilometers

VICTORIA
1851

Canberra
made capital,
1927

TASMANIA 1856

Settlement, 1830–1950

▉	Settled 1830
▓	Settled 1831–1850
▒	Settled 1851–1875
░	Settled 1876–1900
□	Settled 1901–1950

Explorations and New Colonies

In 1824, explorers struggled overland to the coast where Melbourne is now. Robert Burke and William Wills were the first white people to trek all the way from the southern edge of the continent to the north. Unfortunately, they starved to death on the way back. Many other explorers met similar fates or simply disappeared without a trace.

Each exploration led to an influx of new settlers. Explorers reached Adelaide, at the mouth of the Murray River, in 1830. South Australia became a colony in 1836, with Adelaide as its capital. Meanwhile, settlers arrived on the west coast and started the colony of Western Australia in 1829.

In New South Wales, sheep farming was getting to be a big business. Always looking for bigger and better pastures, farmers opened up grazing lands south of the Murray River. That region became the colony of Victoria in 1851. In 1859, the northern part of New South Wales split off to become the colony of Queensland.

Meanwhile, the little island south of Victoria, called Van Diemen's Land, held

A view of Adelaide in 1845
by Samuel T. Gill

some of Australia's most infamous prisons. The island's name was officially changed to Tasmania in 1856 when it became a colony.

In the 1850s, Australia's population almost tripled, from 400,000 to 1.1 million people. As settlers took over more land, they pushed the Aboriginals off their homelands. Those who fought back were shot. Thousands of Aboriginals were killed in these clashes, and diseases brought by the settlers killed more thousands.

The Last of Her People

Tasmanian Aboriginals were once the southernmost people to inhabit the Earth. They died out in the 1800s, mainly from battling white settlers and becoming infected with their diseases. A woman named Truganini, believed to have been the last full-blooded Tasmanian Aboriginal, died in 1876. In 1976, her skeleton was released from a Hobart museum and cremated in Oyster Cove, her birthplace.

In 1997, a delegation of Aboriginals traveled to Europe to recover valuable relics. Edinburgh University in Scotland returned the hair of Truganini. From an English museum, they got back a bracelet and shell necklace that may have been Truganini's. The Truganini Reserve, just outside of Hobart, is named for her.

The Gold Rush

One day in the 1890s, a preacher's wife in Arizona got a rude surprise. On the kitchen table was a note from her husband saying he had taken off for Australia to dig for gold.

While California's gold rush was in full swing, Australia had one of its own. In 1851, gold was discovered in New South Wales and Victoria. First Australians, then thousands of gold seekers from overseas, rushed in to make their fortunes.

California's gold was mostly gold dust, but the gold finds in Australia were huge. The famous Holtermann nugget weighed more than 200 pounds (91 kg)!

In the following decades, more gold was found in Queensland and the Northern Territory. New South Wales turned out to be rich in copper, and Tasmania had tin. Silver was the mineral of the 1880s. The 1890s brought Western Australia's own gold rush, with the Kalgoorlie and Coolgardie goldfields gaining worldwide fame. Thousands of miles of railroad tracks were laid in the 1870s and 1880s. That made it easy to get both minerals and wool to the port cities.

Hordes of ragtag gold hunters headed into the outback with their shovels. Many died in the search. Some, like the Arizona preacher, gave up and went home. Others settled down and became farmers or worked in other people's mines.

Australia's gold rush

The New Nation

As Australia's mother country, Great Britain made the rules and regulations for its colonies. But Britain was distant from Australian affairs. Many residents wanted to form their own government. Then they could make their own decisions about trade, immigration, and defense.

Conventions were organized in 1891 and 1897. Delegates drew up a Constitution, and colonists voted their approval. On January 1, 1901—the first day of the twentieth century—the new federal government took its place. The colonies became states, while the wild Northern Territory remained a territory.

As a new nation, Australia was organized as a constitutional monarchy. The British monarch remained the head of state in Australia. The monarch's governor-general acted on the monarch's behalf. In practice, the british monarch has almost no authority in Australia. The monarch serves primarily as a reminder of the historical relationship between Great Britain and Australia. There is a growing movement in Australia to change the country's constitution, replacing the monarchy with a president as the head of state.

Australia welcomed workers for its farms, mines, and new manufacturing industries. Most immigrants came from England, Scotland, and Ireland. Wary of its Asian neighbors, the new government established a "White Australia" policy. Nonwhites, especially the Chinese, were firmly excluded.

On January 1, 1901, the new nation witnessed the swearing-in of its first governor-general—John Adrian Louis Hope, 7th Earl of Hopetown.

World Wars

When Great Britain entered World War I (1914–1918), it called on Australians to join up. ANZAC—the Australia and New Zealand Army Corps—made its mark in the Dardanelles campaign of 1915. The day the troops landed at Gallipoli, April 25, is still celebrated as a national holiday in Australia. Wartime meant good business for Australia's textile, iron, and steel industries. Wool, beef, and mutton sold well, too.

Australians rose to the challenge again in World War II (1939–1945). In North Africa, they successfully defended the city of Tobruk, Libya, from the Germans. Australians also played a decisive role in the battle of El Alamein, Egypt, in 1942.

Even before that, however, the war arrived at Australia's back door. Fighting broke out in the Pacific when Japan bombed Pearl Harbor, Hawaii, in December 1941. In February 1942, the Northern Territory's capital of Darwin was bombed. U.S. general Douglas MacArthur set up headquarters in Australia, and the two countries fought together in many Pacific campaigns. The Battle of the Coral Sea was one of their major victories.

As before, the war boosted

Australian soldiers on their way to fight in World War II

Australia's economy. The nation's factories turned out ammunition, airplanes, machine parts, and chemicals. Industries welcomed both men and women as workers. The state capitals swelled as rural residents moved in for jobs.

Embracing the Wider World

After the war, Australia relaxed its immigration policy. Refugees from war-torn Europe began to arrive, adding a multicultural flavor to the larger cities. War in Southeast Asia brought another wave of immigrants in the 1970s, and the old White Australia policy was abandoned in 1973.

Vietnamese shop owners in Melbourne

Today, Australia's population is a mix of immigrants and native peoples.

Australia also increased trade with Asian nations, especially those around the Pacific Ocean. Japan, Taiwan, Singapore, Malaysia, and other Pacific Rim countries became important import and export partners. Japan now receives about one-fourth of Australia's exports.

Modern Issues and Concerns

Today, Australia enjoys one of the world's healthiest economies and highest standards of living, but an economic recession struck in the late 1980s and early 1990s. Businesses across the country suffered, and many companies laid off workers or closed down completely. As jobs became scarce, the recession revived the old question of immigration.

The 1990s also brought drought, coupled with fires raging through forests and across the ranges. Millions of acres of forest and grazing land were destroyed.

In 1993, Aboriginals won the right to make claims to tribal lands taken from them since 1788. Opposition has been fierce, as farmers and miners feared the loss of their holdings. Since the Native Title Act, Aboriginals have made many successful claims. Often the agreements call for joint use of a piece of land.

A wave of excitement swept the country when Sydney was chosen as the site of the Summer Olympic Games for the year 2000. It was not just that the games would bring billions of dollars into the economy. It was the glory—the thrill of hosting the first Olympics of the new millennium.

As the old century draws to a close, one of the hottest political issues is independence. An increasing number of Australians want their country to become a wholly independent republic, with an Australian as head of state. They look to the new century as the century of the Australian Republic.

The Political Layer

While the Commonwealth of Australia has existed as a nation since 1901, Australia has kept honorary ties to Great Britain. Not many people think of Australia as a monarchy. But Queen Elizabeth II of Great Britain is also the Queen of Australia and Australia's head of state. Her role, however, is mainly ceremonial. Her representative in Australia is the governor-general.

AUSTRALIA'S BOND TO Great Britain seems destined to be broken. Many Australians are pro-monarchy, but in the 1990s, the cries for independence have grown stronger. The target date is the year 2001—the 100th anniversary of the federal government. It's likely that a national president would then replace the governor-general. In any case, the basic structure of Australia's government will probably remain the same.

The Parliament building in Canberra

The government of Australia is similar to the governments of Great Britain and the United States. As in the United States, governing power in Australia is divided between the federal government and the state governments. There is also a balance of power among three branches of government— executive, legislative, and judicial.

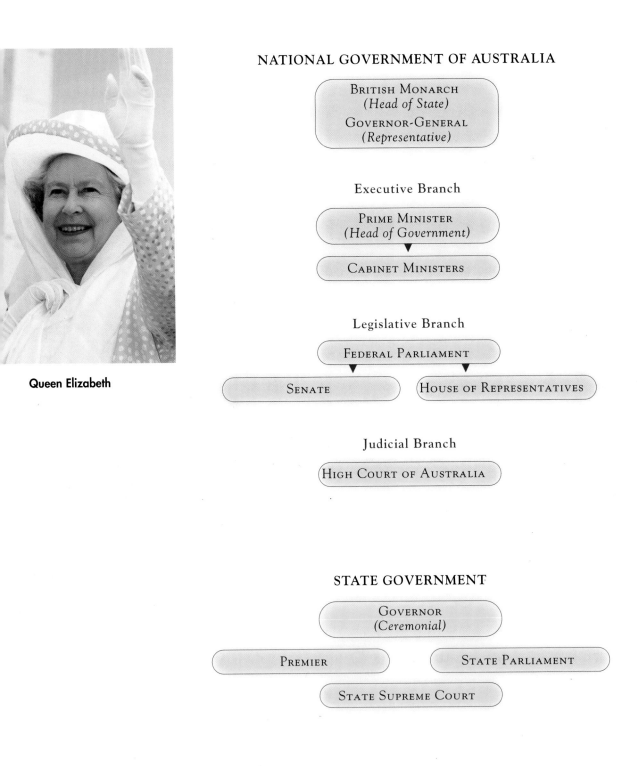

Queen Elizabeth

NATIONAL GOVERNMENT OF AUSTRALIA

BRITISH MONARCH
(Head of State)

GOVERNOR-GENERAL
(Representative)

Executive Branch

PRIME MINISTER
(Head of Government)

CABINET MINISTERS

Legislative Branch

FEDERAL PARLIAMENT

SENATE

HOUSE OF REPRESENTATIVES

Judicial Branch

HIGH COURT OF AUSTRALIA

STATE GOVERNMENT

GOVERNOR
(Ceremonial)

PREMIER

STATE PARLIAMENT

STATE SUPREME COURT

The Executive

Australia's prime minister is the head of government and the nation's chief executive. Like Great Britain, Australia has a parliamentary system of government. In this type of system, the prime minister is the leader of the majority party, or group of parties.

The House of Representatives

Here is how the prime minister is selected. In a general election, members of one party win the majority of the seats in the House of Representatives. The leader of the winning party becomes the new prime minister. That person remains in office until the party chooses another leader or until a different party gains the majority. Sometimes two or more parties band together, forming a coalition party. The leader of a winning coalition becomes prime minister, just as a single-party leader would.

Soon after an election, the prime minister selects members of Parliament to be ministers of various government departments. These officials make up the prime minister's cabinet.

The Parliament

The country's legislature, or law-making body, is the national Parliament. Its upper house is the Senate, and its lower house is the House of Representatives. Members of Parliament are called MPs and senators.

The Aboriginal Flag

Australia's Aboriginals adopted their own flag in 1972. In the center is a golden disk. It represents the sun, the giver of all life. In the background, the top half is a field of black and the bottom half is red. Black stands for the dark-skinned native people, and red is the color of the earth. This flag is recognized popularly but not officially.

Voters elect twelve senators from each state and two from each mainland territory, for a total of 76 senators. Senators serve six-year terms. The 148 members of the House of Representatives are elected from districts according to population. Representatives serve three-year terms. However, the prime minister has the right ask the governor-general to dissolve the Parliament and call for new elections.

Australia's first Aboriginal judge, Bob Bellear

The Courts

Australia's courts make up the judicial branch of government. In making their decisions, the courts interpret and apply Australian law. Many of the country's laws are based on centuries-old British common law.

The High Court of Australia, the nation's highest court, decides cases that involve how the constitution should be interpreted. The High Court also hears cases appealed from lower courts. Each state has various levels of courts, with a state supreme court at the top.

Searching for a National Anthem

Australia conducted a national song poll in 1974 and a referendum in 1977 to see what song Australians would like to have as their national anthem. "Waltzing Matilda" received about 1.8 million votes, and "God Save the Queen" racked up about 1.2 million. The winning song, though, was "Advance Australia Fair," with 2.7 million. Written in 1878, it became the official national anthem in 1984.

Advance Australia Fair

Australians all, let us rejoice,
For we are young and free;
We've golden soil and wealth for toil;
Our home is girt by sea;
Our land abounds in nature's gifts
Of beauty rich and rare;
In history's page, let every stage
Advance Australia Fair.
In joyful strains then let us sing,
Advance Australia Fair.

Beneath our radiant Southern Cross
We'll toil with hearts and hands;
To make this Commonwealth of ours
Renowned of all the lands;
For those who've come across the seas
We've boundless plains to share;
With courage let us all combine
To Advance Australia Fair.
In joyful strains then let us sing,
Advance Australia Fair.

State and Local Governments

Politically, Australia is divided into six states and two mainland territories. Each of these units has a governor, a premier, and a parliament. The governor represents the British monarch. The head of government in a state or territory is the premier, or chief minister. Elected members of the state parliament are the lawmakers. State and territorial governments are in charge of public schools, road building, local police, and public health. They get most of their operating money from the federal government.

Australia's local governments are shires (counties) and cities or towns. Most are governed by an elected council.

Australian Prime Ministers

Name	Dates Served	Party	Name	Dates Served	Party
Edmund Barton	1901–1903	Protectionist	Robert G. Menzies	1939–1941	United
Alfred Deakin	1903–1904	Protectionist	Arthur Fadden	1941	Country
John Christian Watson	1904	Labor	John Curtin	1941–1945	Labor
George H. Reid	1904–1905	Free Trade	Francis M. Forde	1945	Labor
Alfred Deakin	1905–1908	Protectionist	Ben Chifley	1945–1949	Labor
Andrew Fisher	1908–1909	Labor	Robert G. Menzies	1949–1966	Liberal
Alfred Deakin	1909–1910	Fusion	Harold E. Holt	1966–1967	Liberal
Andrew Fisher	1910–1913	Labor	John McEwen	1967–1968	Country
Joseph Cook	1913–1914	Liberal	John G. Gorton	1968–1971	Liberal
Andrew Fisher	1914–1915	Labor	William McMahon	1971–1972	Liberal
William M. Hughes	1915–1917	Labor	Gough Whitlam	1972–1975	Labor
William M. Hughes	1917–1923	Nationalist	Malcolm Fraser	1975–1983	Liberal
Stanley M. Bruce	1923–1929	Nationalist	Robert Hawke	1983–1991	Labor
James Scullin	1929–1932	Labor	Paul Keating	1991–1996	Labor
Joseph A. Lyons	1932–1939	United	John Howard	1996–	Liberal
Earle Page	1939	Country			

It's said that the local governments handle the "three Rs"—rates, roads, and rubbish—that is, collecting various fees, maintaining roads, and picking up garbage. They also take care of public libraries, fire prevention, tourism publicity, recreation sites, and parking regulations.

Voting—It's the Law

By law, Australian citizens who are at least eighteen years old must vote. In federal elections, Australian voters use what is called the preferential system. That is, in marking their ballots, they don't vote for just one candidate. Instead, they number the candidates in order of preference—first choice, second choice, and so on. This way, people who voted for "losing" candidates still have a voice in their government. In a close election, minority parties may form a coalition that proves to be stronger than the leading party.

Traveling polling booths stop at remote areas so people can vote.

Political Parties

Australia has three major political parties. The Liberal Party of Australia favors private enterprise with a minimum of government regulation. The Australian Labor Party (ALP), founded in 1891, is closely allied with trade unions. Its members support government control of factors that affect people's working conditions. The National Party of Australia used to be named the Country Party. It emphasizes the needs of people who live outside the metropolitan areas.

Other parties are the Australian Democratic Party and the Communist Party of Australia. The Green Party's special focus is environmental issues.

In national elections, the Liberal and National parties often form a governing coalition. Labor Party leaders Robert Hawke and Paul Keating, however, served as prime minister from 1983 to 1991 and 1991 to 1996, respectively. This was the longest continuous term of a Labor Party government in Australia's history.

John Howard of Australia's Liberal Party

In the 1996 elections, the Liberal-National Coalition was able to take the lead from the ALP. Liberal Party leader John Howard then became prime minister, and the National Party leader took the office of deputy prime minister.

Canberra

Canberra (left), the nation's capital, is the main part of the Australian Capital Territory. Lake Burley Griffin, named after Canberra's designer, cuts the city in half. On the lake's south side, within the Parliamentary Triangle, are the main government buildings. The point of the triangle is the Parliament Building on Capital Hill. Two legs of the triangle extend from this point and cross the lake— Commonwealth Avenue and Kings Avenue. Other buildings on the south bank are the High Court Building, the National Library, the Australian National Gallery, and several foreign embassies.

Canberra's business section lies north of the lake. Its center is City Hill, in Vernon Circle. A tree-lined boulevard called Anzac Parade leads to the Australian War Memorial. This massive, Byzantine-style monument is the second-most-visited site in the country, after the Sydney Opera House. It traces Australia's part in wars from 1860 to the present.

Canberra was founded in 1913, twelve years after the federal government began, but it took many years to plan and build the city. Parliament held its first session in Canberra in 1927, and the new Parliament House opened in 1988.

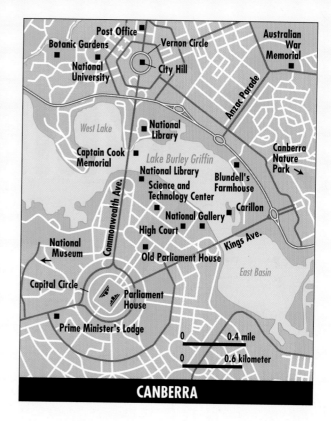

CANBERRA

Making a Living

Sheep and cattle range across the spacious grasslands of the outback. Big livestock farms are called stations, and their farmhouses are called homesteads. Jackaroos (ranch hands) tend the herds, either on horseback or on motorcycles. There are female ranch hands, too—called jillaroos! Some farmers have started to take in tourists to bring in needed income in hard times.

Opposite: **A cattle drive in northeast Victoria**

Sheep and Cattle Stations

SHEEP SAILED TO AUSTRALIA ON THE FIRST BRITISH FLEET IN 1788. Now Australia's sheep population is second only to the flocks in the former Soviet republics. About three-fourths are bred for their wool, and Merino sheep produce the finest wool. Australia is one of the world's top exporters of wool, mutton, and lamb.

Shearing sheep is tiring work.

Shearing time is the year's biggest event on a sheep station. The shearers use electric clippers to shave the fleece off the sheep. They try to remove it in one continuous piece. One large Merino sheep can yield as much as 18 pounds (8 kg) of fleece.

Australian cattle are lean because they're pasture-fed rather than grain-fed. They get lots of exercise, and they don't live on fattening grains. Their meat has about half the fat content of U.S. beef.

Most cattle stations are in north and central Australia. There the land is so dry that a herd needs an immense grazing area to get enough to eat. Some cattle stations are as big as small European countries.

Money Facts

The basic unit of currency in Australia is the Australian dollar (A$). There are 100 cents to a dollar. Paper money comes in denominations of 5, 10, 20, 50, and 100 Australian dollars. Coins are 5, 10, 20, and 50 cents and 1 and 2 dollars.

Crops: In Second Place

Farming activities take up about 60 percent of Australia's total land area. About two-thirds of this land is used for grazing, while the rest is planted in crops. Over half the nation's farmland is in two states—Queensland and New South Wales.

Wheat is Australia's most important grain crop, followed by barley, sorghum, rice, and oats. Sugarcane stalks and leaves are crushed to make hay. Potatoes, tomatoes, and carrots are the main vegetables.

Lush vineyards in New South Wales

The National Gemstone

The opal was selected as Australia's national gemstone in 1993. Often called "fire of the desert," opals glisten with flashing colors. An Aboriginal legend says that opals were created when a rainbow fell to the earth. About 95 percent of the world's precious opals come from the desert regions of central Australia.

Grapes, apples, and bananas are the major fruit crops. The grapes are made into fine wines for local use and export. Oranges, pears, peaches, melons, and pineapples are also produced.

Melons are still harvested by hand.

Mining

Almost all the opals in the world come from Australia. The country is a top diamond producer, too. But precious stones take second place to Australia's valuable minerals.

Gold hunters overran Western Australia in the 1890s. Now the state produces iron ore, nickel, lead, and gold. Its Pilbara region has the nation's richest iron mines. Bauxite, copper, silver, and coal come from Queensland, while New South Wales produces coal, lead, and zinc.

Opals are mined in isolated regions of southern Australia.

What Australia Grows, Makes, and Mines

Agriculture (in Australian dollars)

Livestock slaughtered	$6,271,400,000
Wool	$3,263,900,000
Wheat	$3,263,900,000

Manufacturing

Pig iron	7,554,000 metric tons
Cement	6,397,000 metric tons
Meat processing (beef and veal)	1,706,400 metric tons

Mining

Iron ore	136,991,000 metric tons
Bauxite	42,308,000 metric tons
Zinc	918,000 metric tons

Every year, millions of tons of these minerals travel by rail to the coastal ports for export to countries halfway around the world. Coal is Australia's number-one export, followed by gold.

Victoria is the major oil- and gas-producing state. Most of its oil comes from offshore oil rigs. Some oil and gas comes from South Australia and Western Australia, too.

The nation's mining industry has plenty of problems. It's terribly expensive to mine in Australia. Mining areas are usually far from civilization, so mining companies may have to build new roads, railroads, and even towns. Since the Native Title Act of 1993, the government has to consider any native claims to a piece of land before granting mining leases. This has slowed down the exploration of new mining sites.

Manufacturing

Most of Australia's factories are in Victoria and New South Wales. They make chemicals, heavy machinery, motor vehicles, household appliances, and various other items containing steel.

Some of Australia's factory goods are food products. Vegetables, fruits, sheep, and cattle are processed into an assortment of packaged goods. Other farm products are made into textiles and shoes.

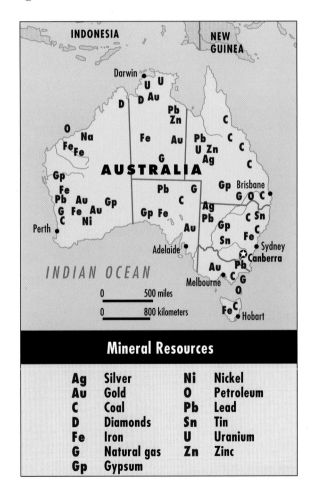

Mineral Resources

Ag	Silver	Ni	Nickel
Au	Gold	O	Petroleum
C	Coal	Pb	Lead
D	Diamonds	Sn	Tin
Fe	Iron	U	Uranium
G	Natural gas	Zn	Zinc
Gp	Gypsum		

From Camels to the Ghan

In the 1840s, the government of Western Australia offered a reward to anyone who would import camels. By the 1890s, thousands of camels had arrived. But railroads, trucks, and cars eventually put them out of business.

Now the Afghan Railway runs along an old camel route between Adelaide and Alice Springs. Called the Ghan for short, it's named after the Afghan camel drivers. The Ghan makes its 20-hour run once or twice a week.

The Ghan is one of Australia's luxury trains for long-distance travel. Another is the Queenslander, which runs from Brisbane to Cairns in 32 hours. But the longest trip of all crosses the entire country. Running from Sydney on the east coast to Perth in the west, the Indian Pacific Railway takes 65 hours!

The longest rail line is the Trans-Australian Railway. Most of Australia's railroads haul farm and mining products into port cities along the coast. Western Australia's iron mines, for instance, rely heavily on freight trains.

Subways and commuter trains serve passengers in Sydney and Melbourne. Several cities used to have trams, or electric

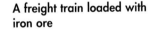

A freight train loaded with iron ore

cable cars that run on city streets. Today, only Melbourne and Adelaide still have tram systems.

Roads and railroads tend to radiate out from Australia's large port cities and state capitals. This pattern developed in the 1800s, when the colony depended mainly on trade with England. Today, national highways run between the state capitals. Paved roads reach many of the larger cities in the interior, too. For much of the outback, though, dirt roads are the rule.

Kangaroos and Doctors in the Sky

Qantas Airlines, with its flying kangaroo symbol, is Australia's only international passenger airline. Its "parent," dating from 1920, was the Queensland and Northern Territory Aerial Services. Put its initials together, and you have Qantas! Other

A Qantas jumbo jet

The Royal Flying Doctor Service saves lives.

international airlines fly in and out of the country, too. For travel within Australia, Qantas and Ansett Airlines provide service to the outback, flying to areas that may be impossible to reach by land.

If people in the outback have a medical emergency, they can call on the Royal Flying Doctor Service (RFDS). This nonprofit service flies in, picks up the patient, and heads for the nearest hospital. Founded in 1928, the RFDS now serves an area of

Making a Living **81**

Sir Reginald Ansett

Reginald Ansett (1909–1981) was born in Inglewood, Victoria, where his father owned a bicycle-repair shop. Reginald worked for a while as a surveyor in the Northern Territory, but it was too lonely. In 1936, he painted "Ansett Airways" on the side of a Fokker airplane and began making daily flights between Hamilton and Melbourne. Ansett Airways became Australia's largest private airline. In 1957, Ansett bought Australian National Airways and then acquired Queensland Air Lines and Butler Air Transport. Ansett Air Freight was formed in 1979. Ansett has now added some international routes to its schedule.

over 2 million square miles (5.2 million sq km). A similar service operates only in the Northern Territory. There are more than 400 airports or airfields throughout the country. Sydney's airport is the busiest, followed by Melbourne's.

Communication

Australia's first newspaper was the government-owned *Sydney Gazette* and *New South Wales Advertiser*. Its first issue appeared in 1803. Today, all of Australia's newspapers are privately owned. Many that were once independent now belong to large media companies.

Most daily newspapers circulate only in their own state. The most widely read daily papers are Melbourne's *Herald Sun* and New South Wales's *Daily Telegraph*. Weekly papers with local news are popular in remote areas. Periodicals that are read nationwide include the daily newspapers *The Australian* and the *Australian Financial Review* and the weekly magazines *The Bulletin*, *Time Australia*, and *Business Review Weekly*.

Rupert Murdoch

Media giant Rupert Murdoch was born in Melbourne in 1931 and attended Oxford University in England. His career began when he inherited the *Adelaide News* from his father in 1954. Its circulation soared when he began featuring sensational stories with gigantic headlines. The same technique worked with Murdoch's three London newspapers and the *New York Post*. He acquired Fox Studios and Fox Television in 1985. Today Murdoch's News Corporation Limited is an international empire of newspaper, book, magazine, TV, and movie companies.

The government-funded Australian Broadcasting Corporation (ABC) operates about 550 radio stations. Fourteen of them send short-wave broadcasts overseas in nine different languages. The ABC has a national television network, too. No commercials run on ABC radio or TV stations. In addition, Australia has 166 commercial radio stations and 44 commercial TV stations. Unlike the ABC stations, the commercial stations need to run ads to make an income.

Faces from Many Places

Australia counts its people every five years. In the 1996 census, the nation had about 18 million people. If they were spread out evenly across the country, there would be only 6 people on every square mile (3.7 per sq km) of land.

I

IN REALITY, THOUGH, AUSTRALIANS ARE SPREAD OUT VERY *un*-evenly. About 80 percent of the population live in the southeastern part of the country. On the other hand, only 4 percent of the people live in the outback, which covers 80 percent of the nation's land area.

To outsiders, Australia might conjure up romantic images of life in the outback. But most Australians are city dwellers. About 85 percent of the people live in urban areas.

Australia's Largest Cities (1996)

Sydney	3,741,290
Melbourne	3,138,147
Brisbane	1,488,883
Perth	1,244,320
Adelaide	1,045,854

A view of Sydney from under the harbor bridge

Cities

Australia's biggest cities are also state capitals. Sydney, the capital of New South Wales, is Australia's largest city, with a 1996 population of about 3.7 million. Next in size is Melbourne, the capital of Victoria, with about 3.1 million people. Next are Brisbane, Perth, and Adelaide. Canberra, the nation's capital, is the sixth-largest city.

Australia's Bosnian and Herzegovinian community during festival time

The Ethnic Mix

In its early days, Australia encouraged immigration. New-comers helped settle the land and provided needed labor. But most of the people admitted to the country were British, Scottish, and Irish. When Australia became a nation in 1901, the new government adopted a "White Australia" policy.

After World War II, however, Australia began to welcome immigrants from other nations. Many came from Lebanon, Greece, Yugoslavia, Hungary, Czechoslovakia, and South America. Today, Melbourne is home to the largest Greek community outside of Greece itself.

In the 1970s, refugees from Southeast Asia poured in. They came from Vietnam, Laos, Cambodia, and neighboring countries. All barriers on the basis of race were removed in 1973. Today most new immigrants are Asians.

Only three-fourths of the people who live in Australia today were born there. The largest group of foreign-born people came from the United Kingdom (England, Scotland, and Wales), Ireland, and New Zealand. Others came from Italy, the former Yugoslavia, Vietnam, Greece, and Germany. Some came from China, Hong Kong, Macao, the Netherlands, Malaysia, and the Philippines. And newcomers from the Middle East include many Arabic-speaking people, as well as Turks, Kurds, and Iranians.

Indigenous People

About 2 percent of the population are indigenous people whose ancestors lived in the area for tens of thousands of years. Most are Aboriginals, but a small number are Torres Strait Islanders. More than half of both these groups live in New South Wales and Queensland. In the Northern Territory, indigenous Australians make up almost one-fourth of the population. They have a strong presence in Western Australia, too.

Who Lives in Australia?

White	95.2%
Other	2.0%
Aboriginal	1.5%
Asian	1.3%

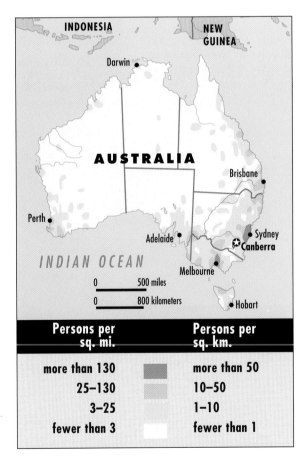

Persons per sq. mi.		Persons per sq. km.
more than 130		more than 50
25–130		10–50
3–25		1–10
fewer than 3		fewer than 1

Aboriginals have seen many changes in their communities over the years.

Ethnically, Australia's Aboriginals are in a class by themselves. Their skin tone ranges from light brown to black, and their hair may be straight, wavy, or curly. Settlers called the Aboriginals "black" and assumed they were related to Africans. But it's more likely that the Aboriginals' ancestors came from Asia.

Australia did not count full-blooded Aboriginals in its census until 1966. The following year, Aboriginals were granted citizenship, and voting rights came in 1984. But it's hard to undo 200 years' worth of damage. Well-meaning missionaries used to take Aboriginal children from their homes, give them English names, and insist that they speak only English. In a recent survey, 10 percent of Aboriginals reported that they'd been removed from their natural families.

Aboriginals today are working to get better housing, education, employment, and health care. They suffer a high rate of untreated diseases and infant deaths. On average, Aboriginals can expect to live to their early forties, while the national average is around eighty years.

Native Land Claims

Aboriginal reserves have been set aside for Australia's native people, but they're rather small compared to the Aboriginals' original territory—the whole continent! The 1976 Aboriginal Land Rights Act was a big step toward correcting the imbalance, however. Among other things, it assigned more than one-fourth of the Northern Territory to the Aboriginals.

Aboriginal elders pass on their traditions to the young.

Edward Mabo

Edward Koiki Mabo (1936–1992) was a native community leader and human-rights activist. His lawsuit for native land rights led to a landmark High Court ruling in 1992. For the first time, the court recognized that indigenous land ownership existed in Australia before Europeans arrived.

Mabo was born on Mer, one of the Murray Islands in the Torres Strait. He worked to improve health, housing, and education for his people. Mabo founded the Black Community School in Townsville, the first institution of its kind in Australia.

In 1993, indigenous Australians won the right to make territorial claims in the nation's courts. Actually, it was the lawsuit of a Torres Strait Islander, Edward Mabo, that led to the new policy. Under the Native Title Act of 1993, indigenous people can claim as much as 10 percent of Australia's total land area.

Language

English, Australia's official language, came in with the first British settlers. But, over time, the accent and vocabulary have gone through some changes. For example, the long *a* sound approaches the sound of a long *i*. Thus, "mate" tends to be pronounced as "mite" and "day" as "die." So the typical Australian greeting "G'day, mate" might sound more like "G'die, mite"!

Australians call their dialect *Strine*. That's a shortened version of "Australian" ("Au-strine"). They call themselves Aussies, and they call their country Oz (as in "Oz-tralia").

Australian Words and Expressions

barbie	barbecue	**jumper**	sweater
bikie	motorcycle rider	**lollies**	candy, sweets
billabong	waterhole in a dry riverbed	**mate**	buddy, pal
bloke	man	**never-never**	the very remote outback
boomer	male kangaroo	**no worries**	It'll be all right.
bunyip	mythical spirit-animal of the bush	**Oz**	Australia
chemist's	drugstore	**sunbake**	sunbathe
fair dinkum	really, honestly	**walkabout**	long, rambling trip
g'day	hello	**water biscuit**	cracker
jumbuck	sheep (above)	**wog**	the flu
		wowser	spoilsport

Many British terms are used in Australian English, such as lift (elevator), petrol (gasoline), and telly (television). Early settlers added new words for unfamiliar plants and animals and, in some cases, they picked up an Aboriginal word.

A busy street along the Gold Coast in Queensland

More than 250 Aboriginal languages existed before the Europeans arrived. Many of them disappeared as their native speakers died out. Today, only about one-fifth of the Aboriginals can speak their native tongue. Aboriginal cultural groups are now working to preserve their languages. They meet with older people who may be the last surviving speakers of a dying language. After collecting all the information on a language, they teach others to speak it.

Well-Educated Children

Children in Australia are well educated compared to children in other countries. In the early 1990s, a United Nations study of schooling around the world found that 100 percent of Australian children reach the fifth grade. In the United States, only 96 percent make it that far. (The world average was 68 percent.) Ninety-nine percent of the Australian people can read and write English.

Australian children must attend school between the ages of six and fifteen. (In Tasmania, attendance is required through age sixteen.) About 75 percent of school-age children

A farming family

attend free public schools. Each state and territory operates its own school system, using funds from the federal government. Most of Australia's private schools are run by the Roman Catholic Church. The national government also provides some support to private schools.

Elementary school lasts six to eight years. Secondary schools add another five or six years of education. However, about one-third of the students drop out of school after their legal requirement is up. Most students who finish secondary school go on to college.

Australia's first colleges were the University of Sydney (founded 1850) and the University of Melbourne (1853). Today, the country has over thirty colleges and universities. They fall into three categories: universities, colleges of advanced education, and technical colleges.

In the past, the regular public-school system tended to overlook Aboriginal children. A new policy begun in 1988 aims to bring more Aboriginals into the public schools. Special programs now teach students about Aboriginal culture, too.

Schools of the Air

Children in the outback often live far away from regular schools. They get their education on the Schools of the Air, talking with their teachers over a two-way radio.

Schools of the Air were set up in 1951 for children from ages six through eleven. Twenty-six Schools of the Air now operate throughout the outback, with about 2,000 students. The teachers are specially trained to run a "classroom" over the air waves. Daily class sessions last an hour and a half, and a dozen students may be tuned in at once.

Opposite: **In today's Australian schools, Aboriginal culture is included in the curriculum.**

Ways of the Spirit

It's sometimes said that "no religion" is Australia's major religion. In the 1996 census, a full 25 percent of the population answered the religion question with "no religion"—or didn't answer the question at all. But religion has played a central role in Australia's history. And freedom of religion is a cornerstone of Australia's constitution.

Opposite: **An Aboriginal tree sculpture**

Christianity

I N COLONIAL TIMES, MOST WHITE AUSTRALIANS BELONGED to the Church of England, or Anglican Church. Irish immigrants brought Roman Catholicism to Australia, and Catholic immigrants from Italy and Asia added to their numbers.

St. Peter's Anglican Cathedral in Adelaide

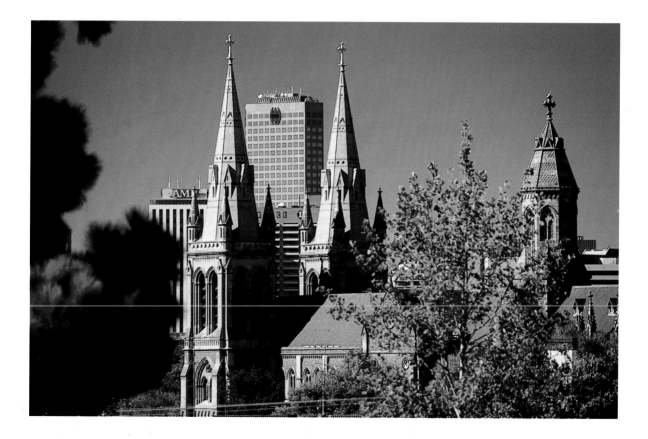

Anglicans and Catholics are still the largest Christian groups. In the late 1980s, Catholics outnumbered Anglicans for the first time. Australia's 1996 census counted about 4 million Anglicans and 4.8 million Catholics.

The Uniting Church is Australia's third-largest religious group. It was formed in 1977 when most of the country's Methodists, Presbyterians, and Congregationalists merged into one church. Other Christian denominations include Baptists, Lutherans, Pentecostals, and members of the Churches of Christ. Missionaries of many denominations still play an active role in Australia.

A Broad Religious Mix

After World War II, waves of immigrants brought an interesting mix of new religions into the country. Most of Australia's large Greek community belongs to the Greek Orthodox Church. Since the 1970s, the number of Buddhists has risen

A Buddhist nun outside a Vietnamese temple in Sydney

as more and more Asians arrived from Vietnam, Laos, Thailand, and Tibet.

Camel drivers brought the faith of Islam to Australia in the 1800s. Whites called the camel drivers Afghans, but not all of them came from Afghanistan. Some came from Pakistan and India. Today, Muslims—followers of Islam—are a fast-growing religious group in Australia. Many newcomers from the Middle East and southern Asia are Muslims.

Religions of Australia	
Catholic (Roman and non-Roman)	26.8%
Anglican	21.8%
Uniting Church	7.5%
Orthodox	2.8%
Other Christian	11.4%
Muslim	1.1%
Buddhist	1.1%
Jewish	0.4%
Hindu	0.4%
No religion	16.5%
Not stated	8.7%

Jewish people were among the first settlers to sail to Australia in 1788. Today, Australia's Jewish community numbers about 80,000 people, mainly from European countries where Jews have been persecuted. The Great Synagogue in Sydney is the country's major Jewish house of worship.

Australia seems far from Europe's tragic Holocaust, in which the Nazi regime exterminated 6 million Jews. But Australia was one of the countries in which Jewish people resettled for safety. Ironically, some Nazi war criminals saw Australia as a safe haven, too. In 1993, an alleged former Nazi was tried in South Australia for war crimes against Jews. A state Supreme Court jury found him not guilty after deliberating for less than an hour. This landmark case left the Jewish community deeply disappointed and discouraged.

Only a few gifted artists can paint Dreamtime images on tree bark.

The Dreaming

Before Europeans arrived, the Aboriginals enjoyed a rich, free-flowing spiritual life. Daily activities and the world of nature were charged with the life of the spirit.

The Dreaming, or Dreamtime, is central to the Aboriginals' belief system. The Dreaming is the spiritual realm that existed long before the world began. Mythical beings of the Dreaming

created the land and all plants, animals, and humans. They set down the laws of nature and the rules for orderly living. Then they were absorbed into the landscape. Dreamtime beings continue to energize all of nature and serve as the guiding force in everyday life.

Each clan honored its own totems. Totems were symbols such as plants, animals, ancestors, or Dreaming beings. An animal totem stood for all the powerful qualities of that species. Clan members might refrain from eating their totemic animals or plants. Natural sites such as hills or rock formations could also be totems. In Aboriginal mythology, a spiritual creature may have transformed itself into one of these landforms.

Through their totems, people kept in touch with nature and with the Dreaming. Totemism also gave the clan pride and a sense of unity. A distant group might have an entirely different set of totems. Thus, the "others" fell short of being truly human.

Aboriginal women conducting a religious ceremony for newborns called baby-smoking

Religious rituals were a vital part of Aboriginal life. People spent weeks planning and preparing for a ceremony. Some rituals were complex dances with music and chants. Performers were often adorned with body paint and headdresses. Artists made bark paintings and carved wooden totems to use in ceremonies, too. For an Aboriginal boy, an important ritual was

his initiation into the secrets of adult male life. Women and girls had their own secret rituals, too.

As Aboriginals lost their land, they also lost touch with their religion and culture. "If you take our land," said an elder of Arnhem Land, "you take our soul."

Rock art is still an integral part of some initiation rites.

Arts and Fun

Where did AC/DC, Men at Work, INXS, the Bee Gees, the Little River Band, Midnight Oil, Olivia Newton-John, and Helen Reddy come from? Australia, of course! They all started out in Australian music clubs, then went on to worldwide fame.

Opposite: **Aboriginal art is intricate and colorful.**

Ever since the Beatles played in Australia in the 1960s, rock music's popularity has exploded. Young people in Australia hear the latest pop music on radio and TV and in discos. Pop concerts in the cities draw huge crowds, just as they do in Europe and the Americas.

The main concert hall in Sydney's famous Opera House

The Classical Scene

Some famous classical musicians have come out of Australia, too. Composer Percy Grainger (1882–1961) wrote charming versions of British folk tunes. Dame Nellie Melba was an international opera star in the 1890s. Another opera singer, Dame Joan Sutherland, began to catch the world's attention in the 1960s.

The Australia Council, a government agency, supports the national Australian Opera and Australian Ballet. It also sponsors hundreds of other cultural groups and arts festivals throughout the country. Audiences

The Sydney Opera House

Ask non-Australians to name a famous building in Australia, and they'll probably pick the Sydney Opera House. This massive arts complex is the busiest art center in the world. Over 40 million people have visited the Opera House since it opened in 1973. With its soaring, pointed arches looming over Sydney Harbour, it's a stunning piece of modern architecture. The Opera Theatre and 2,700-seat Concert Hall are just two of its nine hundred separate enclosures. Others are rehearsal studios, dressing rooms, restaurants, bars, and reception halls.

fill the massive Sydney Opera House for operas, ballets, and plays, as well as orchestra and chamber music concerts.

Each state capital has its own symphony orchestra, managed by the Australian Broadcasting Corporation (ABC). The ABC also broadcasts the orchestras' concerts and features international music stars in concerts. Each state is proud of its own opera and dance companies. The Australian Ballet, the Sydney Dance Company, and the Victoria State Opera have all enjoyed successful tours in other countries.

Dame Nellie Melba

Nellie Melba (1861–1931) was Australia's greatest opera star. Born Helen Porter in Richmond, near Melbourne, she chose the stage name of Melba in honor of Melbourne. She made her international debut in Brussels, Belgium, in 1887. A London debut followed in 1888. She made her first appearance at New York's Metropolitan Opera in 1893 as Lucia in *Lucia di Lammermoor*. Melba had a magnificent singing range of 3½ octaves. In 1918, she was named a dame of the British Empire, an honor similar to knighthood for men. The dessert Peach Melba is named for her.

Aboriginal Music and Dance

For the Aboriginals, music and dance are centuries-old rituals. Some dances mimic the movements of animals, while others tell ancient myths and spiritual tales. The Aboriginal and Islander Dance Theatre performs many types of traditional Aboriginal music and dance.

A hollowed-out wooden tube called the *didjeridoo* is a traditional musical instrument. Music-makers may beat out rhythms with sticks, clubs, or boomerangs or beat on a skin stretched over a frame. Aboriginal songs include sacred chants

An Aboriginal playing the didjeridoo

with hundreds of verses. A tribe traditionally described its territory through songs, instead of maps. Simple songs for entertainment may consist only of short verses or repeated phrases. Music and dance are an important part of *corroborees*, the Aboriginals' group get-togethers.

The Silver Screen

Paul Hogan's acting career began when he hosted an Australian TV show. Now he's best known as the star of

Mel Gibson

Mel Columcille Gerard Gibson was born on January 3, 1956, in Peekskill, New York. At the age of 12, he moved to Sydney with his family. He attended the National Institute of Dramatic Arts in Sydney and later joined the South Australia Theatre Company. Gibson first became famous for his roles in *Mad Max* and *The Road Warrior*. He earned the Australian Film Institute's

Best Actor award for his performance in *Gallipoli*. After three *Lethal Weapon* movies, Gibson directed, produced, and starred in *Braveheart*, which won five Academy Awards. Gibson, one of eleven children, has six children of his own.

Paul Hogan

Paul Hogan is best known as the fearless, free-spirited hero of *Crocodile Dundee* movies. He was born on October 8, 1939, in Lightning Ridge, New South Wales. Among his many odd jobs, he worked as a chauffeur, a boxer, and a rigger on the Sydney Harbour Bridge. In the 1970s, Hogan hosted *The Paul Hogan Show* on Australian TV. He wrote the screenplays for both *Crocodile Dundee* films and received an Academy Award nomination for Best Screenplay in 1986. Paul Hogan's other movies include *Flipper* (1996), *Lightning Jack* (1994), and *Anzacs: The War Down Under* (1985).

Errol Flynn

Errol Leslie Thomson Flynn (1909–1959) was a wildly popular Hollywood actor of the 1930s and 1940s. Born in Hobart, Tasmania, Flynn was a mischievous child. He recalled that his mother used to call him a "wicked, wicked boy." On screen, Flynn portrayed a romantic hero and a swashbuckling adventurer. His 50 movies include *The Adventures of Robin Hood*, *Captain Blood*, *The Sea Hawk*, *They Died with Their Boots On*, and *The Sun Also Rises*.

Crocodile Dundee. This 1986 adventure movie set in the bush was the most popular Australian film ever made. But Australians have produced many others.

Peter Weir's *Picnic at Hanging Rock* (1975) was one of the first Australian films to gain worldwide attention. Weir followed with the World War I movie *Gallipoli* in 1981. Bruce Beresford's *Breaker Morant* came out in 1980. Director George Miller made *Mad Max* (1979) and *The Road Warrior* (1981). Baz Luhrmann's *Strictly Ballroom* (1992) was another popular Australian film.

Art Traditions

Early Aboriginal people painted with ocher, a reddish-orange mineral ground up and mixed with water. They painted everyday scenes or mythical figures on tree bark, wood, and rock. Typically, the figures were drawn in "X-ray" style, showing their bones and inner organs. Some paintings discovered on cave walls and rock faces are 25,000 years old.

Today, Aboriginal artists produce beautiful paintings in their traditional style. Aboriginal children are learning their native art traditions, too. Through school and community

Well-known artist Sheila Brim and her work

programs, artists teach them the ancient techniques and symbols. Storytelling is an important part of the process. As the artists work, they tell stories about the creatures they're painting and what they mean.

In the 1800s, Australian artists painted in the Impressionist style, which was popular in Europe at the time. In the late 1800s, a group of these artists became known as the Heidelberg School. It was named after the suburb of Melbourne where they worked. Their subjects were shimmering, haunting landscapes and pastoral scenes. Tom Roberts, Frederick McCubbin, and Sir Ernest Arthur Streeton were some of the best-known Heidelberg artists.

Some of Australia's greatest modern painters are Russell Drysdale, Sidney Nolan, and Frederick Williams. Nolan painted fantastic scenes from Australian folklore. Drysdale and Williams specialized in scenes of the outback.

Albert Namatjira

Albert Namatjira (1902–1959) was Australia's most famous Aboriginal artist. A member of the Aranda tribe, he grew up on the Hermannsburg Mission near Alice Springs. Namatjira used watercolors to portray the scenic beauty of the outback. His European-style paintings appealed to white art collectors, and he used the proceeds to help his fellow tribe members.

With government funding for the arts, many cities have built excellent art museums. Australia's national art museum is the National Gallery of Australia in Canberra. It includes a large collection of Australian art, as well as masterpieces from around the world.

Francis Greenway, Convict and Architect

Francis Howard Greenway made good use of his time in Australia's penal colony. A talented British architect, Greenway was sentenced to fourteen years in prison for forgery. Transported to Australia in 1814, he soon caught the eye of Governor Lachlan Macquarie. Macquarie put him in charge of designing and building all government construction projects. Greenway's strong, simple style is now called Australian colonial architecture, and his buildings are among the most beautiful in the country. Examples are St. James's Church and Hyde Park Barracks, at the north end of Sydney's Hyde Park.

Summer Droving by
Sir Ernest Arthur Streeton

Marcus Clarke

In Australia's early years as a colony, Europeans liked to read about its exotic landscapes and wildlife. They devoured the writings of Australian explorers and naturalists. The first Australian novel was *Quintus Servinton*, published in 1831. The author, Henry Savery—a convict himself—describes life as a convict. The same theme runs through Marcus Clarke's powerful novel *His Natural Life* (1874). It tells the wretched story of a convict in an Australian prison colony.

In the late 1800s, life in the Australian bush was a common subject. "Bush ballads" and short stories about bush life were published in the weekly *Bulletin*, called the "bushman's Bible." Some of its finest pieces were bush stories by Henry Lawson and the ballad "Waltzing Matilda," by Andrew ("The Banjo") Paterson.

Waltz of the Banjo Man

Andrew Barton Paterson (1864–1941) was born in the bush near Bathurst, New South Wales. He was a lawyer, a newspaper reporter, the editor of the *Sydney Evening News,* and a World War I ambulance driver. He signed his poems as "The Banjo."

Paterson is best known and loved for his bush ballad "Waltzing Matilda." It tells the tale of a swagman (wandering laborer) sitting by a billabong (waterhole) heating up his billy (tea) over the campfire, singing, "You'll come a-waltzing, Matilda, with me." Along came a jumbuck (sheep), and he stuck it in his tucker-bag (food sack). Then came a squatter (sheep farmer) with troopers to arrest him. The swagman swore they'd never take him alive. Into the billabong he sprang, singing, "You'll come a-waltzing, Matilda, with me." And if you pass by, you can still hear him sing....

Patrick White is called the greatest modern Australian writer. His most famous novels are *The Tree of Man, Voss,* and *Riders in the Chariot.* White won the Nobel Prize for literature in 1973.

Novelist Thomas Keneally was interested in the way one individual can effect great events in history. His novels include *The Chant of Jimmie Blacksmith* (1972) and *Schindler's Ark* (1982). When it was published in the United States, *Schindler's Ark* was retitled *Schindler's List.* It became the basis for Stephen Spielberg's haunting film.

Sports

Australians start playing team sports in elementary school. They never seem to outgrow their sports fever. Every town has amateur sports teams, and fans crowd the stadiums to cheer their favorite professionals.

British and Australian rugby players compete at Sydney's football stadium

Luc Longley

Lucien James "Luc" Longley was born in Melbourne in 1969. Both of his parents played basketball. Luc began playing basketball at age twelve. He played with Australia's national basketball team in the 1988 and 1992 Olympic Games. When Longley joined the Minnesota Timberwolves in 1991, he became the first Australian to play in the National Basketball Association (NBA). Joining the Chicago Bulls in 1994 as a center, he helped them win the 1996, 1997, and 1998 NBA championships. Longley stands 7 feet 2 inches (218 cm) tall.

Evonne Goolagong Cawley

Tennis legend Evonne Goolagong Cawley, a Wiradjuri Aboriginal, was born in 1951 in Barellan, New South Wales. As a teenager, Evonne was stung by occasional racist comments from other players. But she believed in being a good sport and kept her spirits up. A strong player with great timing, she seemed to play with little effort. Cawley won the Wimbledon tournament twice, the Australian Open four times, and the French Open once.

Cricket, a ball-and-bat game, was traditionally a popular pastime for the British upper class. (The saying "It's not cricket" means "That's unfair" or "That play is not in line with the rules of cricket.") Settlers brought cricket to Australia, where it's now the most popular team sport of the summertime.

Rugby, another British import, is sort of a cross between soccer and American football. Rugby league is the professional form, while rugby union is the amateur version. Rugby league is wildly popular in Queensland and New South Wales. Another kind of football game is association football, or soccer. Australia's rugby and soccer teams play against the teams of other countries all over the world.

Australian Rules Football, or "footie," is uniquely Australian. The first game took place in Melbourne in 1858. The Grand Final—like the Super Bowl in the United States—is one of the biggest sports events of the year.

The Melbourne Cup horse race has been running every year since 1861. Held at 2 P.M. sharp on the first Tuesday in November, it draws fans from around the world. The event is so popular that it's the occasion for a public holiday in Victoria.

Greg Norman: The Shark

Professional golfer Greg Norman was born in Mt. Isa, Queensland, in 1955. Nicknamed the Great White Shark, Norman won two British Open titles, five Australian Opens, and dozens of other tournaments. He has suffered some notable losses, too. "What keeps me going," Norman says, "is that I love the game with a passion." To encourage and teach young golfers, he established the Greg Norman Golf Foundation in Queensland.

Camels race in Australia, too, bringing excitement to many local festivals. The Camel Cup race is held every year in Alice Springs.

The Camel Cup in Alice Springs

Aussies Win the America's Cup

It was a glorious day for Australia when the 12-meter sloop *Australia II* won the America's Cup on September 26, 1983. Under skipper John Bertrand, the Aussies were the first challengers to claim the cup from U.S. yachtsmen in the race's 132-year history. Australians had tried unsuccessfully for the cup in 1962, 1967, 1970, 1974, 1977, and 1980. The cup returned to the United States in 1987, when Australia's *Kookaburra III* lost to the U.S. challenger *Stars & Stripes*. New Zealanders won in 1995. Auckland, New Zealand, is the site for the America's Cup in the year 2000.

Australia's warm climate makes a good setting for golf, tennis, and track. The Australian Open tennis tournament dates back to 1905. Some of Australia's tennis stars are Evonne Goolagong Cawley, Margaret Smith Court, and Rod Laver.

Dozens of Australians have brought home medals from the Olympic Games. But the Olympic event Australians may never forget is the Summer Olympics of the year 2000. Sydney was chosen to host the international spectacle. To house the events, the city has built an Olympic Stadium and several other world-class facilities. But remember—North America's summer is Australia's winter. The start date was set for September. Weatherwise, that's like March in the Northern Hemisphere.

Olympic Champs

In the 1996 Summer Olympics, Australians won 9 gold medals, 9 silver medals (including Louise McPaul, right, for the javelin), and 23 bronze medals. They gave some of their top performances in track and field, cycling, swimming, and rowing. In the 1992 Olympics, Aussies tallied up 7 gold, 9 silver, and 11 bronze medals.

The country's sunny, sandy beaches are great for swimming, surfing, boating, and yachting. Sydney's Bondi Beach is the most famous beach in Australia. It's jammed with surfers (called surfies), musclemen, and sunbathers. Australia produces some top-notch surfers and hosts championship surfing tournaments.

Surfboat races are exciting events. The crews row out to markers and back to shore, battling treacherous breakers. The Australia Cup is one of the world's most prestigious yacht races. The popular Sydney–Hobart yacht race on December 26 is one of the toughest ocean races in the world.

Surfboat racing is an exciting but dangerous sport.

How People Live

The vast majority of Australians live in urban areas. However, their housing patterns are different from those in other big cities around the world. City dwellers in Australia have more living space. They don't have to live in tightly packed high-rise apartment buildings.

Residential parts of the city are called suburbs and look much like the suburbs in other countries. Most residents live in a single-family house with a yard. Typically, there's a barbie (barbecue) in the backyard. Even in the city, wildlife is never far away. Snakes, possums, and even hungry kangaroos are likely to drop by.

Inner suburbs, those nearest to the city center, used to be poor areas. But people have been cleaning up the inner cities and rebuilding them as middle-class residences. One example is Paddington, or Paddo, in Sydney's inner city. It has become quite a classy neighborhood with its renovated Victorian homes.

Roundabouts and Bulldust

Australians drive on the left side of the road, so all vehicles have the steering wheel on the right. In cars with manual transmission, the stick shift is to the driver's left.

You need special vehicles to drive through Australia's outback.

At some big intersections, traffic is channeled into a roundabout, or traffic circle. In the United States, drivers head around to the right (counterclockwise) to get through these circles. In Australia, drivers circle to the left (clockwise).

Driving in the outback is an adventure in itself. Four-wheel–drive vehicles are the best way to travel. Even then, drivers are likely to run into bulldust. Bulldust is fine, powdery dust that fills a deep hole in the road. It's impossible to tell when a patch of bulldust is coming up. Your first clue is finding yourself wheel-deep in a hole. If you're driving a four-wheeler, you stand a better chance of getting out.

Life in the Outback

The outback, Australia's vast interior, has a culture of its own. It's tough to live there. Much of the land is arid, dusty, and drought-stricken, with the sun beating down mercilessly. Thousands of hopeful prospectors headed to the outback during the gold rush. Now, sand-covered ghost towns, aban-

A typical outback café

doned mines, and makeshift cemeteries show where they lived and died.

Farming and mining are the main activities in the outback. For hardworking miners, the mining towns offer stores for their basic needs. Then there's the town pub—a much-needed place for camaraderie, storytelling, and bragging about a bright future.

Sheep and cattle stations, like the mines, are usually a long drive from the nearest town. Ranchers might drive into town once a week to pick up food and supplies and take care of any business. Cattle roundups and sheep shearing are the high points of the year.

Youngsters in the outback have lots of space for roaming around and exploring. They're close to animals, too—farm animals, pets, and wild animals. Instead of spending all day at school, they spend an hour and a half a day with Schools of the Air. Homework is due only once a week!

National Holidays

January 1	New Year's Day
January 26	Australia Day
	(Captain Phillip's 1788 landing)
March or April	Easter
April 25	ANZAC Day
Early June	Queen Elizabeth's Birthday
December 25	Christmas
December 26	Boxing Day

Long-Distance Medical Care

Snakebites, motorcycle accidents, and heatstroke happen every day in the outback, but getting good medical care can be difficult. If someone needs to be rushed to a hospital, they can radio the Royal Flying Doctor Service (RFDS).

Opposite: **Body painting is an art that has been handed down from one generation to the next.**

Most ailments are easier to treat, though. Every homestead has a kit of basic medicines, each identified by a number. For nonemergencies, people call the RFDS and describe their symptoms. Then the RFDS calls a doctor, who prescribes the proper medicine by number.

Aboriginals: Juggling Two Ways of Life

About two-thirds of Australia's Aboriginal people have assimilated into white culture. They live and work in cities, on farms, or on mining sites. In the outback, they may live on Aboriginal reserves or in scattered towns. Tribal councils make important decisions for a group, and tribal elders are respected for their wisdom and spiritual insight.

A few Aboriginal groups live as they have for centuries. They live off the land, hunting with spears and *woomeras*

Videoconferencing in the Outback

In the high-tech medium of videoconferencing, the Warlpiri are far ahead of most communities. These Aboriginals in the Northern Territory's Tanami region own and operate their own network. The Tanami Network was up and running in 1993. It now links four Warlpiri settlements and sites in Sydney, Darwin, and Alice Springs.

Participants speak to each other "face to face" using a video camera and a color-TV screen that captures the hand gestures important in Aboriginal communication. Through the network they attend classes, consult with doctors, and find out about government services. Aboriginal artists use the network to show their work, too.

The Aboriginals even have videoconferences with indigenous people in other countries. In one meeting, they exchanged native dances with the Little Red Cree nation in Alberta, Canada. Most contacts, however, are personal or ceremonial. People use the network to keep in touch with distant family and friends. Aboriginal leaders also use the video network to meet and make decisions.

Some Boomerangs Don't Come Back

Aboriginals have used boomerangs for thousands of years. The oldest-known boomerang, found in South Australia, is 10,000 years old. The crescent-shaped instrument is carved from wood and often painted with animals and other designs. It can be used for hunting, fighting, or beating out dance rhythms. When thrown properly, it returns to the thrower. But boomerangs are not always designed to return. Some are just a type of hunting club. They drop to the ground after striking an animal. Cultures in India and Egypt also used curved hunting clubs, but only Australian Aboriginals had a returning type.

(spear throwers) and gathering plants. Periodically, several clans meet in *corroborees* and perform traditional dances.

Regaining their land rights has opened up more opportunities for the Aboriginals. Tourists in Australia often want to visit Aboriginal sites and observe native arts and culture. In the past, non-Aboriginals managed—and profited from—these expeditions. Now Aboriginals are beginning to take control of their own tourism industry. Some organize their own tours, while others work as guides or interpreters in jointly managed national parks. This way, they can present their culture in an authentic way and protect their sacred sites.

Most Aboriginal children attend primary school—in towns, on sheep or cattle stations, or over the airwaves. For secondary school, they may attend a boarding school or take correspondence courses. But many don't go beyond primary education. Girls in some tribes may marry at thirteen or fourteen years old.

In case of illness, Aboriginals seek modern medical care. But they often put more trust in their *ngangkari* than in the doctor. The ngangkari is part doctor and part priest. He understands the spiritual problem underlying an illness and performs rituals to relieve it.

Food from the Land

Cattle and sheep farms supply Aussies with plenty of beef and lamb. Chicken ("chook") and pork are popular, too. Meat, potatoes, and vegetables make up a regular, everyday meal, but Australia's many immigrant communities spice up the basic fare. Big cities now offer a tasty choice of Greek, Italian, Indian, Chinese, Japanese, Vietnamese, and Thai restaurants.

A seafood market in Adelaide

Australia abounds with seafood. More than 1,500 species of fish from coastal waters end up on the table. Shark, whiting, and sea trout are favorites, as are shrimp, oysters, and enormous crayfish. Tasmanian crabs weigh as much as 30 pounds (14 kg). Moreton Bay bugs are small and tasty crayfish.

Fresh tropical fruits are plentiful. Queenslanders are called banana-eaters because there are so many banana trees there. Other fruits include pineapples, paw-paw (papayas), mangoes, and passion fruit. They're eaten fresh, used in cooking, and made into fruit juice. Fruits from the bush include the *quandong* (a wild peach) and the native cherry of New South Wales.

Native wild animals find their way to the table, too. Emu meat is said to taste like turkey, and kangaroo meat is tender and low in cholesterol.

The Story of Vegemite

Fred Walker knew that yeast was nutritious. He wanted his food company in Melbourne to make it in some delicious form. One day in 1922, Fred asked Dr. Cyril Callister, the company scientist, to come up with something. Callister brewed up a pasty mixture of yeast extract, celery, onions, and other ingredients. Fred held a competition to find a name for the new product, and the winner was "Vegemite." During World War II, Vegemite was included in military rations. It became so popular that, for a time, there was a Vegemite shortage. Vegemite-eating experts warn against eating it by the spoonful. Instead, spread butter on bread, then smear Vegemite in with the butter. Bon appétit!

Opposite: **Karijini National Park, a perfect escape from hectic urban life**

How to Eat Like an Aussie

A typical brekkie (breakfast) consists of eggs and snags (sausages). Hearty eaters prefer a plate of steak, pork chops, and snags. Snags cooked in egg batter are called "toad in the hole." Lunch might be a sanger (sandwich) or fish and chips (french fries). But put vinegar on the chips. Tomato sauce (catsup) goes on meat pies. A meat pie in pea soup or gravy is called a floater.

Looking for some milk? Don't go to a milk bar—that's a general store. If you want strong black tea, ask for "billy." Noncarbonated soft drinks are called cordials, while "soda" means carbonated water. Lemon squash is lemonade, icy poles are popsicles, and lollies are candy and sweets.

Vegemite (commonly known in the United States by the brand name Marmite) is Australia's multipurpose snack food. It's a gooey brown yeast and vegetable paste that's slightly softer than creamy peanut butter. Aussies spread Vegemite on bread, toast, and crackers. Even babies eat it as a "starter" food. Rich in B vitamins, it's good for cell growth, nerves, skin, and eyes.

Food for the Soul

"We'll throw another shrimp in the barbie for you," an Australian travel ad used to say. They just might. Barbies, or barbecues, are a favorite social event. They can happen anytime, anywhere. People barbecue at home, on the beach, in the bush, and in parks and picnic areas. Some restaurants and bars provide meat and let the customers grill it themselves.

As cities and suburbs are getting crowded, more people use their free time to "go bush." They spend a weekend or even a couple of weeks bushwalking—that is, trekking and camping in the bush. Some bushwalkers bring food supplies, while others take the "survival" route. They hunt animals for food and cook them over a campfire.

Under the starry sky, the silence is enormous, broken only by the cries of wild things in the bush. Yet there are those who swear they hear more. Is it the song of a long-dead wanderer? Or the faint murmurs of ancient spirits of the land?

Timeline

World History

c. 2500 B.C. Egyptians build the Pyramids
and Sphinx in Giza.

563 B.C. Buddha is born in India.

A.D. 313 The Roman emperor Constantine
recognizes Christianity.

610 The prophet Muhammad begins preaching
a new religion called Islam.

1054 The Eastern (Orthodox) and Western
(Roman) Churches break apart.

1066 William the Conqueror defeats
the English in the Battle of Hastings.

1095 Pope Urban II proclaims the First Crusade.

1215 King John seals the Magna Carta.

1300s The Renaissance begins in Italy.

1347 The Black Death sweeps through Europe.

1453 Ottoman Turks capture Constantinople,
conquering the Byzantine Empire.

1492 Columbus arrives in North America.

1500s The Reformation leads to the birth
of Protestantism.

Dutch navigator Willem Jansz becomes   1606
the first European known to set foot
on Australia.

Abel Janszoon Tasman lands on   1642
Van Diemen's Land. It was
later renamed Tasmania.

Captain James Cook arrives in   1770
Australia aboard The Endeavor.

Australian History

Captain Arthur Phillip arrives in Botany Bay with the first shipload of prisoners from Great Britain. — 1788

Robert Burke and William Wills become the first white people to trek from the southern edge of the continent to the north. — 1824

Australia's gold rush begins in New South Wales and Victoria. — 1851

Great Britain stops transporting its prisoners to Australia. — 1868

Australia becomes an independent nation. — 1901

Australia's capital moves from Melbourne to Canberra, a federal district. — 1927

Australia's constitution is amended to allow federal programs to benefit Aboriginals. — 1967

The Northern Territory becomes responsible for its own administration. — 1978

"Advance Australia Fair" becomes Australia's national anthem. — 1984

Aboriginals win the right to make claims to tribal lands taken from then since 1788. — 1993

World History

1776 — The Declaration of Independence is signed.

1789 — The French Revolution begins.

1865 — The American Civil War ends.

1914 — World War I breaks out.

1917 — The Bolshevik Revolution brings Communism to Russia.

1929 — Worldwide economic depression begins.

1939 — World War II begins, following the German invasion of Poland.

1957 — The Vietnam War starts.

1989 — The Berlin Wall is torn down, as Communism crumbles in Eastern Europe.

1996 — Bill Clinton is reelected U.S. president.

Fast Facts

Official name: Commonwealth of Australia

Capital: Canberra

Official language: English

The Sydney Opera House

The Australian national flag

Official religion:	None	
Anthems:	"Advance Australia Fair" (national); "God Save the Queen" (royal)	
Government:	Constitutional monarchy; in practice, a parliamentary democracy with two legislative houses	
Chief of state:	British monarch, who is also monarch of Australia; in practice, governor-general, who performs functions in the monarch's absence	
Head of government:	Prime minister	
Area:	2,978,147 square miles (7,713,364 sq km)	
Coordinates of geographic center:	27° 00' S, 133° 00' E	
Dimensions:	Australia extends approximately 2,500 miles (4,025 km) from east to west and about 2,300 miles (3,700 km) from north to south.	
Bordering countries:	Australia is separated from Indonesia in the northwest by the Timor and the Arafura Seas; from Papua New Guinea in the northeast by the Torres Strait; from the Coral Sea Islands Territory also in the northeast by the Great Barrier Reef; from New Zealand in the southeast by the Tasman Sea; and from Antarctica to the south by the Indian Ocean.	
Highest elevation:	Mount Kosciusko, 7,310 feet (2,228 m)	
Lowest elevation:	Lake Eyre, 52 feet (16 m) below sea level	

Average temperatures:

	in July	*in January*
Sydney	78°F (26°C)	61°F (16°C)
Canberra	82°F (28°C)	52°F (11°C)
Darwin	90°F (32°C)	87°F (30°C)

Average annual rainfall:	Sydney	48 inches (123 cm)
	Canberra	25 inches (63 cm)
	Darwin	65 inches (167 cm)

National population (1996): 18,287,000

Population (1996) of largest cities in Australia:	Sydney	3,741,290
	Melbourne	3,138,147
	Brisbane	1,488,883
	Perth	1,244,320
	Adelaide	1,045,854

Famous landmarks:

▶ *The Sydney Opera House* attracts worldwide attention because of its dramatic setting on the Harbour and its sail-like architecture.

▶ *Ayers Rock*, a huge loaf-shaped rock formation just south of the MacDonnell Ranges, is a popular tourist attraction in Uluru National Park.

▶ *The Great Barrier Reef* is the world's largest coral reef and one of the country's most popular travel destinations.

Industry: Sheep and cattle ranching are important agricultural activities. Australia is the world's largest producer of wool, mutton, and lamb. Its beef products are shipped around the world. Nearly 60 percent of Australia's total land area is devoted to farming. Major crops include wheat, barley, sorghum, rice, and oats. Australia is rich in minerals, including iron ore, nickel, lead, and gold.

Australian currency

Almost all of the opals in the world are mined in Australia. Most of Australia's factories are in Victoria and New South Wales. They make chemicals, heavy machinery, motor vehicles, and appliances.

Currency: One Australian dollar ($A) equals 100 cents. 1998 exchange rate: U.S. $1=$A 1.26

Weights and measures: Metric system

Literacy: 99%

Common Australian words and phrases:

barbie	barbecue
bikie	motorcycle rider
billabong	waterhole in a dry riverbed
fair dinkum	really, honestly
g'day	hello
jumbuck	sheep
jumper	sweater
lollies	candy, sweets
mate	buddy, pal
sunbake	sunbathe
walkabout	long, rambling trip
water biscuit	cracker

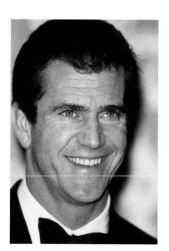

Mel Gibson

Famous People: Evonne Goolagong Cawley (1951–)
Tennis player
Mel Gibson (1956–)
Actor
Thomas Keneally (1935–)
Writer
Greg Norman (1955–)
Golfer
Patrick White (1912–1990)
Writer and winner of 1973 Nobel Prize for literature

To Find Out More

Nonfiction

▶ Allison, Robert J. *Australia*. Austin, Tex.: Raintree/Steck-Vaughn, 1996.

▶ Darian-Smith, Kate. *Australia and Oceania*. Austin, Tex.: Raintree/Steck-Vaughn, 1997.

▶ Darian-Smith, Kate. *The Australian Outback and Its People*. New York: Thompson Learning, 1995.

▶ Dolce, Laura, and Sandra Stotksy. *Australia*. New York: Chelsea House, 1997.

▶ Meisel, Jacqueline Drobis. *Australia: The Land Down Under*. Tarrytown, N.Y.: Marshall Cavendish, 1997.

▶ Morrison, Reg, and Maggie Morrison. *Australia: The Four Billion Year Journey of a Continent*. New York: Facts on File, 1990.

▶ Williams, Brian, and Brenda Williams. *Australia*. Chicago: World Book, 1998.

Biography

▶ Haney, David. *Captain James Cook and the Explorers of the Pacific*. New York: Chelsea House, 1992.

▶ Sirak, Ron. *Greg Norman*. New York: Chelsea House, 1998.

Fiction

▶ Crew, Gary. *Angel's Gate*. New York: Simon and Schuster, 1995.

▶ Zindel, Paul. *Reef of Death*. New York: HarperCollins, 1998.

Folktales

▶ Noonuccal, Oodgeroo, and Bronwyn Bancroft (illustrator). *Dreamtime: Aboriginal Stories*. New York: Lothrop, Lee & Shepard, 1994.

Websites

▶ **Prime Minister's Kids' Page**

http://www.pm.gov.au/pm/kids/kids.htm

Information on Australia for young people

▶ **Embassy of Australia**

http://www.aust.emb.nw.dc.us/

Official website of the Australian Embassy in Washington, D.C.

▶ **CIA World Factbook**

http://www.odci.gov/cia/publications/factbook/country-frame.html

Detailed statistical information on Australia from the U.S. government

Organizations and Embassies

▶ Embassy of Australia
1601 Massachusetts Avenue, N.W.
Washington, DC 20036
(202) 797-3255

Index

Page numbers in *italics*
indicate illustrations.

Meet the Author

Ann Heinrichs fell in love with faraway places while reading Doctor Dolittle books as a child. She has traveled through most of the United States and several countries in Europe, as well as northwest Africa, the Middle East, and east Asia.

An editor for many years, Ann has conducted extensive research on Australia. As project editor for the World Heritage series, copublished by UNESCO and Children's Press, she helped develop English-language manuscripts for *Australia: Land of Natural Wonders*, *Prehistoric Rock Art* (which included many Aborigine sites), and *Coral Reefs* (which included the Great Barrier Reef).

"For this book, I also interviewed several Australians about their experiences in the outback. I attended a digeridoo performance, studied the journals of Captain James Cook, explored the many websites of the Aboriginal and Torres Strait Islander peoples, and paid zoo visits to kangaroos, koalas, wombats, emus, and pythons. And riding a camel in the Sinai Desert gave me a feel for the camelback explorers of Australia's desert interior.

"To me, writing nonfiction is a bigger challenge than writing fiction. With nonfiction, you can't just dream something up—everything has to be researched. When I uncover the facts, they turn out to be more spectacular than fiction could ever be. And I'm always on the lookout for what kids in another country are up to, so I can report back to kids here."

Ann Heinrichs grew up in Arkansas and lives in Chicago. She is the author of more than twenty-five books for children and young adults on American, Asian, and African history and culture. Her book *Tibet*, in Children's Press's Enchantment of the World series, was selected by the International Campaign for Tibet for use in its educational outreach program. *Japan*, in the True Book series, was awarded honorable mention by the National Federation of Press Women.

Ann holds a bachelor's and a master's degree in piano performance. These days, her performing arts are t'ai chi chuan and kung fu sword.

Photo Credits